Letter to a
Great Grandson

Also by Hugh Downs
in Large Print:

My America *(editor)*
On Camera
Thirty Dirty Lies About "Old"

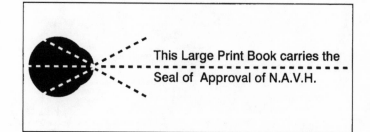

Letter to a Great Grandson

A Message of Love, Advice, and Hopes for the Future

Hugh Downs

Thorndike Press • Waterville, Maine

Published in 2005 by arrangement with Scribner, an imprint of Simon & Schuster, Inc.

Thorndike Press® Large Print Senior Lifestyles.

The tree indicium is a trademark of Thorndike Press.

The text of this Large Print edition is unabridged.
Other aspects of the book may vary from the original edition.

Set in 16 pt. Plantin by Elena Picard.

Printed in the United States on permanent paper.

Library of Congress Cataloging-in-Publication Data

Downs, Hugh.
 Letter to a great grandson: a message of love, advice, and hopes for the future / Hugh Downs.
  p. cm.
  ISBN 0-7862-7237-6 (lg. print : hc : alk. paper)
  1. Men — Conduct of life. 2. Black, Alexander William, 2002– 3. Downs, Hugh. I. Title.
 BJ1601.D69 2005
  170´.44 — dc22   2004063144

To Nikki and Cameron Black,
whose parenting is
more than exemplary.

National Association for Visually Handicapped
serving the partially seeing

As the Founder/CEO of NAVH, the only national health agency solely devoted to those who, although not totally blind, have an eye disease which could lead to serious visual impairment, I am pleased to recognize Thorndike Press* as one of the leading publishers in the large print field.

Founded in 1954 in San Francisco to prepare large print textbooks for partially seeing children, NAVH became the pioneer and standard setting agency in the preparation of large type.

Today, those publishers who meet our standards carry the prestigious "Seal of Approval" indicating high quality large print. We are delighted that Thorndike Press is one of the publishers whose titles meet these standards. We are also pleased to recognize the significant contribution Thorndike Press is making in this important and growing field.

Lorraine H. Marchi, L.H.D.
Founder/CEO
NAVH

* Thorndike Press encompasses the following imprints: Thorndike, Wheeler, Walker and Large Pr int Press.

Acknowledgments

The following people are of extreme importance in the creation of this book:

First, Alexander William Black, the unwitting recipient of the letter the book consists of, who I am certain will at first give it a low priority, deciding not even to read it until some years have gone by.

Second, Johannes (Gänsfleisch zur Laden) Gutenberg, whose famous invention of movable type allowed it to be printed. (It would have been a letter in any case, but not a book.)

Third, Bill Adler, to whom I expressed my desire to write such a letter, and who immediately said, "That would make a book!" (As was the case with Gutenberg, it would have been a letter in any event, but not a book.)

Fourth (there is no particular order in these acknowledgments — a theme carried out in the book itself), Lisa Drew, whose editorial wisdom in matters of style and whose patience and literary advice were invaluable.

Fifth, Erin Curler, whose shepherding of logistics back and forth — in getting manuscript drafts and the inevitable communications regarding details, deadlines, etc., was executed with calm efficiency.

Sixth, Ruth Downs, one of Master Black's four great-grandmothers, but the only one living in the same house as the author, and thus finding herself in a position to give excellent and needed suggestions for thematic material and improvement of expression.

Seventh, Xander's parents, already acknowledged in the dedication, but worthy of being saluted again for creating with apparent ease, a miraculously superior human being — the target of the book, and in the fair and balanced opinion of the author, the hands-down greatest great-grandchild in the history of the human race.

And, of course, whatever merit the book has is due solely to the author, and any errors in it were caused by the above-named people.

Preface

This is not a letter to a little boy. It is a letter to one human male of different ages: a youngster just able to read, a young adult, a middle-aged man, and an old man. If he reads it at each of those four stages of life (and I would like it if he did), he will get something different from it each time.

I grant that at times I appear to be talking to him while he is an infant, and I asked my wife why I would do this. She said, "Simple. It's because he is so *cute*."

Okay.

I can't know the events of his life, but I will be relating many of mine, and interspersing fragments of advice, opinion, prediction (attempts to picture what I think his world will be like at different dates in his lifetime), plus personal feelings.

This document will be long for a letter — short for a book.

I can't mail it into the future, but published books can sit patiently on shelves, and I count on his parents to let him know it exists. I will, of course, personally hand him the first copy, but its chances of surviving the gauntlet all family documents must run to become valuable make its publication desirable. These documents face six steps of evolution: (1) important, (2) filed, (3) forgotten, (4) trash, (5) rediscovered (sometimes), (6) treasured.

The fact that Alexander arrived before I left is very pleasing to me. If I'm still here when he has a family I will qualify as ancient. I would certainly welcome an opportunity to know his children.

— Hugh Downs
Paradise Valley, Arizona
November 25, 2003

Portrait of the recipient as a young man.

Letter to a Great Grandson

Dear Alexander,

Two weeks ago, as I write this, you came into the world, a little astonished and distressed, which is quite natural, considering how we all arrive — naked, cut off from the nourishment of umbilical blood and the warmth and comfort of the womb, and thrown suddenly into a place of bright lights, loud noises, cold air (which must now rush into lungs never before used — air containing, along with nitrogen and some trace gases, oxygen, known to be the most corrosive gas there is), and the harsh new sounds of voices no longer muffled by abdominal walls and amniotic fluid — voices trying to express love and protection, but not immediately recognized as such.

And very soon you were hungry. Without any knowledge of where the restaurants are.

But like all of us at the very beginning, you took it in stride, with the almost infinite capacity newborns have to deal with frustration and discomfort — and the merciful amnesia that keeps it from being so traumatic it scars you for the rest of your life. Nature is kind, basically, and I want you to realize this. At various times in your life you will not think so, but it's true. Only years and years later will

16

you somehow remember that you came here "trailing clouds of glory," and that your home is a cosmos that harbors no hostility toward you. My hope is that you will come to know the truth of this early enough to enhance the quality of your life.

You are actually the first real newborn I ever saw. I gazed on you about seven minutes after you emerged from your mother's insides. When my own children were born I was in a waiting room and didn't get to see them until about a half hour had gone by and they were all cleaned up, and not red and wrinkled. They were very young babies, but no longer newborns. I saw you when you were very little, very unhappy, and very red and wrinkled. But you had a good voice and powerful lungs, which knew how to function the minute you got here. And in less than a half hour you were a clean and hungry baby.

Now, having settled into the routine of your full-time employment — sucking and swallowing, emptying breasts and bottles and filling diapers — you are on the standard track of development. You will gradually come to log the sights and sounds that will allow recognition of faces and voices — your mother's and your father's, and those of others you know to be relatives and friendly — and finding the difference between you and not-you. This is not easy, but you will stumble onto how you can move an arm or leg in the direction you want — in a blinding flash you will know that a desired motion is not coincidence, but that you actually caused it. You can implement volition! It is amazing how early these profound enlightenments occur.

What a fortunate young man you are! This is not something I expect you to appreciate when you first read this. But there are people who come into this world in places and under conditions that put them at tremendous risk of not living long, or living a life of misery — hungry, unloved, diseased, abused, or neglected. Too many of these arrive on earth daily. You have parents who love you, who love each other, and who consider you their highest priority. This will not spoil you. Rather it will allow your development to include a sense of security and a love for yourself — your own existence — that leads to the capacity to love others. And to

feel concern for those less fortunate.

Just Who Am I?

I should explain who I am. You will
know shortly that the two people who
love you and take care of you are
called your parents. (Actually they
will be called Mommy and Daddy,
but it's the same thing.) You have to
have a mommy and a daddy to be
here, and if you're lucky they will
both be around a lot of the time while
you are growing up. In time you will
learn that everybody has to have a
mother and father — even your own
mother and father have mothers and
fathers. This leads to a lot of relatives
and ancestors, most of whom you'll

never know, but you don't need to.

Where was I? Yes. Who I am: I am one of your eight great-grandparents. Your father's mother is my daughter. So my daughter is your grandmother. I contributed twelve and a half percent of your DNA. Another twelve and a half percent was contributed by your great-grandmother Ruth, who is my wife. (I'll have to explain "wife" later.)

Surely your eyes have glazed over by now and I don't blame you. But we are related.

I hope you come to like me, to maybe look forward to visiting me and your great-grandmother Ruth. What you mean to us is more than you can grasp right now, and you won't fully understand until you have been alive for several decades, but you will get a glimpse of it when you have children of your own, and a wider view when you become a grandfather.

And when you are a *great*-grandfather, you will experience something so much more powerful and meaningful than being a father or a grandfather that you will look at the march of generations with new eyes.

What's the Point of This Letter?

I would like you to read this letter as soon as you can read anything — and I would be happy if you read it all as a young adult, and again when you are middle-aged. And if you should go through it again in old age, even if it reveals to you my limitations and causes you to find many of my ideas quaint, I would hope that from the perspective of your world, whatever it is at that time, you will be able to muster some affection for your old ancestor who loved you.

What I hope to do is to present four things for your review: (1) some of my philosophy of life, (2) some biographical material, including stuff about other family members that I believe you will be glad I wrote down, (3) speculation on what your world will be like at different stages of your life, and (4) advice (unasked for, I grant, but possibly useful). If you are true to human nature, you will (a) disagree with the advice and not act on it, (b) agree with the advice and not act on it, or (c) in your mature years, say, "By George, he was right — I should have acted on it."

Quite often I will wonder about some event, or branch of the family tree that I never knew or have forgotten, and I will think for a split second, I'll have to ask Dad (or Gramp) about that. And of course right away I realize I can't ask them. Some cemeteries, as a poet wrote, are filled with the bones of people I'd like to talk to.

I wonder how old you'll be before you understand what you did for my life. I only hope I can do a fraction as much for yours.

Your arrival replucked old resonances — from my own early childhood, and that of my children, and from the childhoods of my grandchildren, one of whom is your father.

When we take you for a jaunt in

your stroller and meet neighbors who are fairly sure we don't have a child your age, and they say, "Oh, is this your grandchild?" we smile and say, "No." Then we explain that you are a *great*-grandchild, and they feel obliged to say that we don't look old enough to have a great-grandchild, and we feel wonderful, our vanity carefully obscuring whatever falsehood might be a component of their politeness. They then get to the proper point and comment on how handsome you are, and then we *really* salute their taste and intellect. It's all very courtly.

Your reaction, from inside your stroller, is one of indifference to the whole conversation. Your mind is, wisely, on other things. Like where your pacifier fell to, or why one sock is half off. It makes a pleasant day.

You're beginning to smile a lot and to laugh occasionally. Is it possible you already sense the comic nature of the human condition? You will be a philosopher.

Naturally I am concerned about your world. You have come into it at a time of some uncertainty and danger. I have to admit I know of few times in history when an infant was born into a time generally considered secure and benign. Maybe during some of the decades of Queen Victoria's reign there was such a time, at least for some citizens of an empire on which the sun never set. (The empire, of course, owed its existence to the exploitation of people for whom the world was not benign.)

My mother (one of your eight

great-great-grandmothers) had reason to be very worried about the
world in the 1930s. With three sons
who were little boys at the time of the
1929 stock market crash, she saw di-
saster ahead. She was right in almost
everything. The banks closed in
1932, the Great Depression came
down on all of the poor and middle-
class and many of the rich. Before it
was over, war clouds had darkened
Europe. She was convinced there
would be a war. Her sons would
surely be involved in it, and it would
be a world war. There hadn't been a
world war since 1918. She was right
about all this. My father probably
worried also, but he was not as vocal
about it, and managed an optimism
born of his tendency to look at history
with a stand-back attitude, distancing

himself from all apocalyptic potential. He had a long enough keel to escape despair in the face of short-term crises.

As it happened, my two brothers and I survived the war, even though all of us were in the military, and so here, through luck, my mother was wrong and had worried for nothing.

Now your parents will worry about you.

Who Can Know the Future?

If I give you advice on how to order your life into the future, of what value is it, you might ask, unless my view of the future is right? But even knowing I can't know the future with any accuracy, some of my advice will be of use — because I do know something about the past. Our country has been built on principles and ideas that we value, though we don't manage to live up to them very well, and in the framework of those principles you can garner a lot of happiness and satisfaction if you take the right road.

You are very lucky to have been born in this country, but you were not born into Utopia. Utopia is not something you need to understand now because there is no such thing.

Here Comes a Chunk of Advice

In your early weeks just eat everything you are offered, at every chance. It will be almost exclusively milk. Maybe a little fuzz off your pacifier that has fallen onto the rug, but the milk from your mother's body has given you enormous immune protections, and you won't be harmed. Be as much of a glutton as you can. There is no danger of obesity at your age. When you are about two months old, your parents may be told to extend the time between feedings if you are getting a bit pudgy, but that is not a problem now. Pay no attention to adults who love you and would give their eyeteeth to see any sign of appreciation or understanding or affection or true humor or consideration and apology for the sleeplessness you cause them. Don't feel guilty about soiling diapers they buy or dousing their clothes or faces with urine during a change. You are at the center of your world, which is where you belong, and everything revolves around you. Do whatever you like. When you want something — anything — holler. Hungry? Holler. Too hot? Holler. Too cold? Holler. Uncomfortable? Too long before you have summoned your servants to see them come running? Too intolerable to remain sitting in your own excrement? Holler. This is part of your job, along with eating and sleeping. You have no employer, no government regulations, no community responsibilities, no reason to feel any impending duties. . . .

But, you poor guy, neither do you yet have any capacity to enjoy the anticipation of good things, or the savoring of past comforts and satisfactions. Good things are either now — in the immediate present — or they

31

don't exist; and generally they don't exist unless they are in your mouth. One other thing, a technique that will make any opposition or annoyance melt away: when you get a handle on facial muscles, try to make your lips wider and have your cheeks pull your mouth into a grin, which will probably produce dimples and give the impression that you are amused. After doing this a few times, you will *feel* amused, because the effect on adults is impressive. They fall apart with admiration and affection. You will follow this with laughter because they will laugh, and laughter will increase your bond with them and your ability to get your way. Keep on with it, and you can reign as sovereign in the household, at least until you get siblings (something I'll explain later).

The landscape will generally be the same until a couple of things unfold. Here is my advice at a somewhat later stage.

Important Advice at a Later Stage

When you are several months older, maybe eighteen or twenty months, you are old enough not only to understand some words but to utter them. Practice saying no to everything. This is a smart move. Up to now, out of the obsequiousness of agreeing with your parents because you crave their favor and approval, you have gone along with whatever they have suggested. You've said yes to everything. But you've finally realized you are in a complicated situation, because you haven't known what you have said yes to. You might have to backtrack if your agreement leads you to something you don't like. But saying no is a much better thing to do. When you say no, you don't have to wonder about what it is you are saying no to: it is a blanket statement. Doesn't matter what there is to say no about — it simply solves the problem by ending the discussion. Since most of what your parents want you to do or not do is contrary to your desires, it is valuable to make a blanket negation of anything they suggest. You should be able to achieve this before the age of two, but at age two you should have it perfected. It will, unfortunately, lead to some confrontations where you will be the loser, but you should not give it up until your third birthday, when you will have learned some other techniques of getting your way. But meantime rehearse the word "no" and use it at every opportunity. It will give you a sense of power and self-importance for a while, until you are bruised enough to consider the possibility that other people have rights and valid opinions, and that you might possibly get your way more often in the long run by yielding to them on occasion.

Now some weeks have gone by (in fact, nine weeks and three days), and I have seen you smile and try to say a word every now and then. You have your own language, which I cannot speak, but you will learn my language before I learn yours, so I don't worry about it.

Three of your four grandparents are living. *Six* of your eight great-grandparents are living. And you have one great-great-grandmother — your mother's mother's father's mother! A great-great-grandmother! I can tell, because we have a picture of the two of you, how thrilled she was to hold you for the first time when you made that trip west to see her! Having a living ancestor of that generation is a twenty-first-century thing. In the past, people rarely knew all four grandparents or any great-grandparents. Having a great-great-grandmother is a real indication that things have changed.

I'm sure the times will have changed a lot more when you are my age.

What Will Things Be Like When You Are Grown?

When you are your father's present age (thirty-three years as I write this) it will be 2035. A third of the twenty-first century will have passed. When you are your grandfather Surles's present age, you will be into the third quarter of the century. And when you are my age you will find yourself in the last quarter of that hundred-year block of time you chose to arrive in. It will be 2083. You will likely live to celebrate the arrival of the twenty-second century. After all, you will only be ninety-eight. There are over sixty thousand centenarians now in the United States. What will the world be like when you join their expanded ranks?

I suspect that among today's prophets neither the optimists nor the pessimists will prove correct in their view of the future.

The optimists will tend to envision a world of peace, a stabilized population, enormous medical advances, a higher percentage of democratized countries, established renewable energy sources, more rapid communication and transportation, and breakthroughs in longevity.

The pessimists will dwell on the risks of high-tech weaponry available to paranoid dictators, uncontrolled diseases ravaging the world's population, and hatred and aggression growing on a planet far too crowded and nearing the exhaustion of resources.

The most likely scenario is somewhere in between.

If wars were to end it would be the first time in scores of centuries. (War as we know it did not exist thousands of years ago — there was violence and tribal strife, but not organized armies or national entities vying for territory or natural resources.) I wish I could offer some rational hope that we might put an end to war, but right now I think it is unlikely.

You are an American, by virtue of having been born here. Will your country still be what it is today when you are an old man? I hope not. I hope by then it will have moved toward a better ability to live according to the excellent principles on which it was founded. I hope it will have reduced injustice and discrimination. I hope it will have taken its place in the community of nations as a leader and an example, admired for its moral strength and not feared and hated for its military and economic strength. I hope it will by then have proved what the great Indian leader Mahatma Gandhi said when asked what he thought of Western civilization: "It would be a good idea." Civilization is a work in progress, and the United States has the opportunity to contribute to its development.

But in spite of wrong paths, setbacks, and discouraging political situations, America is still, on its momentum alone, the greatest potential entity for leading all peoples of the world to better lives. Winston Churchill (half American by his own admission, since his mother was American) once said, "The American people can always be counted on to do the right thing; but only after all the alternatives have been exhausted."

At the moment we are still taking some wrong forks in the road to the future. But this is not a proper reason to despair of that future. Perhaps I envy you a little because of your place in time, and the future you will get to see unfold.

Stages of Life

In prehistoric times people most likely experienced two stages of life: child and adult. In early civilizations there seemed to be four: infancy, childhood, youth, and age. In recent centuries cultures acknowledged seven ages of man: babyhood, child-hood, adolescence, young adulthood, prime adulthood, middle age, and old age.

But now think what discrete cate-gories you will have gone through if you live a long life, and you have a very good chance of doing this. I see seventeen different stages. Let's ex-amine them.

You started as a zygote. (Tech-nically you were a zygote before fertil-ization was complete: the male and the female haploid nuclei had to come together and combine their chromosomes into a single diploid nucleus before you were on your way. If you choose years from now to be-come a medical doctor or a cell re-searcher, you will know much more about this — and by that time there will be much more to know.) You became a zygote with the merger of the sperm and ovum, which pooled their DNA. Your identity was not pinned down until past the stage of development where you could have split apart and become a twin or some other multiple. But once past this point you were a real person. A little later you became an embryo, an established living entity destined to follow the genetic development of a human. After an embryo stage you were a fetus, until your birthday (you only have one birthday; other so-called birthdays are anniversaries). On leaving your mother's body you became, appropriately, a newborn, then a baby, and then an infant.

After being a newborn, a baby, and an infant, you will become a toddler, a small child, a half-grown child, a postpuberty minor (adolescent), a young adult, a prime adult, a young middle-ager, a prime middle-ager, a member of the young old, then of the old old, and finally an ancient. This makes the seventeen ages of man. With a modicum of luck you can span all these ages and enjoy some satisfaction and peace through all of them.

(1) **Zygote.** You are a zygote at the moment of union between egg and sperm, and before they form anything like a primitive multicelled animal. This lasts a week or two.

(2) **Embryo.** An embryo is what you were when the first cell differentiation began to make you look like a living being. This

status is enjoyed for close to two months.

(3) **Fetus.** A fetus is what you are considered by expert and layman alike to be when your form is unmistakably human.

(4) **Newborn.** When you were born you had a brief time of being somewhat wrinkled, under-weight, wretchedly unprepared for a world harsher than the placental environment you had lived in for three-fourths of a year. You were called a "new-born." And you had no reason to forgive those who helped you into this harshness. In fact, you wailed about the injustice. But after a short time you be-came a bona fide baby.

(5) **Baby.** I marveled how you

did this. Nobody taught you how to suck on a nipple, or how to convert breast milk into tissue and nerves and muscle and blood and bones and energy — you did this all by yourself. And you seemed to take it for granted.

At times when you were satisfied and happy you would look at me, and I would look back at you, and each of us was wondering who in the world the other really was. (Of course I know your name and your parents and a great deal of your family tree, and I am proud of my connection with you, but who are you? Where did you come from?)

It is so easy to think of a baby as something that is going to become a human being — mere potential. But this is not the case at all. When I looked squarely into your eyes and saw how frankly curious and honest you were (the academic Scott Buchanan said of the hippie philosophy that said you shouldn't trust anyone over thirty, "People who say you should never trust anyone over thirty are way too conservative — I don't trust anyone over four"), I realized I wasn't looking at a baby. I was looking at a *person* — a very, very young *person*. And a very honest person. You will be completely honest until you are taught to say things like you had a good time when you *didn't* have a good time. People under four, when asked, "Don't you want to say good-bye to Aunt Emma?" will say, "No."

And I knew, as I watched you, that there were things you knew that you wanted to tell me. I could tell by the urgent movements of your arms and legs, and the sounds in your little throat, and the intensity in your gaze that you had something important you wanted to get across to me — but that by the time you could utter words, you might well have forgotten what it was.

This brought me to the realization that you may have a sounder grasp of who we both are than I have. I confess I don't know where I came from, where my daughter (your grandmother) came from, or where her son (your father) came from. Right now you might know more about these things than I do, because you are shortcutting a path to this kind of

Knowing that I am cluttering up with cognitive processes. But I can see in your eyes that you know *something* — a great, secret *something*. And I'd like to know what it is.

This doesn't mean you know everything. You won't know everything until you are eighteen years old. You'll have it all figured out then. Eighteen-year-olds somehow manage this, and it's a great feeling. But eighteen-year-olds are never able to hold on to that complete knowledge of everything. The silver lining is that on losing it, wisdom will begin to bud — but only when it all starts to unravel. Gradually you will accumulate more questions than answers, and you'll come to the realization that the more you learn, the more you expand the periphery of your ignorance. Bummer!

★ ★ ★

You won't mind this if you have one solid piece of ground to anchor in. As myriad certainties evolve into doubts and questions, you can remain secure if there is one thing in your life you know to be true. I'll come to that later. But we are still talking about stages of life and you are still a baby. (Er, I mean a *person*.)

In the next stage you become a very young child, which we can call an infant.

(6) **Infant.** This is the beginning of childhood. The French word *enfance* means "childhood." You will move into this seamlessly, but during the brief time of being an infant you will learn how to turn over,

crawl, coordinate most of your movements, separate the me from the not me, and utter words like "mama" and "dada." You will be heading for Toddlerhood. When you stand upright, holding on to something, you will be jubilant. When you let go and fall in a heap, you will think it is the end of the world.

(7) **Toddler.** While still an infant you will retain all rights and privileges of your age group, and I advise you to exercise them with vigor. You will no longer be an infant when you start to toddle. You will be a Toddler. This should occur around ten to thirteen months, although it varies. If you toddle

early it doesn't mean you have precocious skill — there's no guarantee you won't fall down a lot or become awkward for quite a while. And if you are late getting upright and toddling it doesn't mean you will stumble and bump into the furniture for the rest of your life. It's more complicated than that.

But what a thrill it must be! If we could remember, I suspect we'd recall that the first success in moving around without crawling — actually balancing on two feet and taking steps that get us someplace without inevitably pitching forward onto our face — this must be more of a thrill than learning to ride a bicycle, or soloing an airplane! I will look for the signs of satisfaction and thrill you exhibit when you take those first steps.

Now you will be a toddler, and we've already talked about adding to this glorious mobility the technique you will have of saying no to everything. Your tenure as a toddler should last about a year and a half, when you become a small child. These time periods are mine, and I urge you not to argue with others who set different times and ages on the different stages of life. They are entitled to their opinions, and we must not be intolerant of their unfortunate and deplorable error in disagreeing with your great-grandfather!

(8) **Small Child.** As a small child you will become aware of an

ongoing need for protection. It is normal for you to have a considerable fear of getting lost — separated from your mother or father. You will be mortified if you revert on rare occasion to diaper days and find you have wet your pants. It's not the end of the world. I experienced this coming home from a sort of prekindergarten session where I was ashamed to whisper to the day-care lady that it might be wise for me to visit the bathroom before leaving. It was almost a full block from our house and I almost made it all the way — but not quite. I was four, and somehow knew my parents considered me toilet trained, a fact that added to my humiliation. I cite this, even though it isn't particularly edifying, to let you know that it is not a unique tragedy.

(9) **Half-grown child.** After discharging your duties as a small child you will, without particular effort, suddenly become a half-grown child. Or, I think of it as a standard-size child, who will go through puberty before becoming an adolescent.

When we use the word "child" in English, what usually pops into our head is a picture of an eight-year-old. To call a three- or four-year-old half-grown is misleading. But the term does not refer so much to years as to size. In the matter of height, you'll be halfway to whatever adult height you achieve when you are two. This is hard to accept, but it's true. Your father, whose height your great-grandmother and I measured and marked on an eight-foot board every birthday and many times in between, was a tad over three feet tall when he became two. He is a tad over six feet now and will probably stay that way until he is old, when the discs between his vertebrae and his knee cartilages begin to thin a bit, and then he will be a little less than six feet. So actually at age three you will be more than half-grown height-wise (but, of course, less than half-grown from a standpoint of volume and weight).

School Days

You will, of course, be required to go to school, unless your parents judge the school system to be so worthless they choose to take over your education themselves. But if you do go to a school, you will get some schooling, and hopefully some education along with it. I'm sure your parents will at least make up for the education deficiencies America's school system suffers from. Parents are more responsible for, and provide more, education than schools anyway. A child has an uphill battle if his parents are uninterested in his education, uneducated, or unavailable during those years.

What should you learn? If the school you first go to has a proper idea of this (and it may), I am sure it will expose you to some ideas of how to read, how to count (even if the school has computer terminals for its students that seem to make this unnecessary), and how to absorb a technique for learning these things. That's the most important. If you don't remember one fact but have developed a desire to find out — and a technique for seeking the information you need — your school will have been successful. Hopefully, it will not focus on training you to do well on tests. It will try to impart to you the kindling of inspiration and curiosity, and the tools to pursue knowledge. And I believe that if your schools fail in this, knowing your parents, they will provide you with this important wisdom. And you will respond to it.

You may later (as a teenager) seek to repudiate a lot of what your parents have taught you, and they will seem to have become stuffy and restrictive, but don't worry about that. They'll survive, and so will you.

When you start school I hope you have a better first day than I did. My mother delivered me to the door of Horace Mann School on Jameson Avenue in Lima, Ohio, along with several other parents and a gaggle of children about my age. I knew my way home (four blocks west), but I knew nothing about recess. When what seemed like an interminable session came to an end, all the children were turned out into the school yard and I thought the school day was over. I streaked for home. My mother was horrified to see me and asked why I had come home in the middle of the morning. I told her the teacher said we could go. My escape was short-lived. I was delivered back to school, arriving after the recess period was over, and to my great humiliation, my cheeks flaming, I was handed off to the teacher in front of the class. Being singled out is bad enough under any circumstances, but having a spotlight on you for criminal activities is mangling.

Adults have a bad habit of treating puberty with disrespect. For some reason they find it an amusing stage. This attitude may come from a desire to deny they suffered through it themselves, or faulty memory about the intensity and uncertainty of an important transition. Their disdain and patronizing are an ostrich reflex against the responsibility to be of help. They don't want to talk about sex, they don't want to open any can of worms that could be embarrassing to them, and they feel that sneering and amusement will cushion them against a reality they remember with discomfort.

Puberty is a lonely time, because urges and changes are felt as isolated conditions — conditions that no one else feels or has ever felt. A sense of uniqueness is heightened by the general absence of advice or support from anyone else — peers, parents, mentors.

There are exceptions: I don't recall any time in my own life that I was unaware of the so-called facts of life. Any question I asked was answered by my parents truthfully, and they made no big deal of it — they never volunteered information beyond what I asked but seemed unembarrassed and calm. Once my mother's aplomb was jarred momentarily when I came home from school and asked her what "fuck" meant. I was six years old. She was stirring clothes in a washing machine and I remember that she dropped the stick she was using as though it were a snake, but within two seconds she had recovered her calm. "Where did you hear that word?" she asked. I told her some kids at recess said it and laughed at me because I didn't know what it meant. She told me, as though she were explaining a weather phenomenon or a word like "consolidate." I nodded, not particularly impressed, and went outside to play in the yard with my brother. (At a later age I was surprised that there were contemporaries of mine who didn't know where babies came from.) My parents thus avoided any set talk about the birds and the bees. It was simply unnecessary.

But while this frankness may have helped me in understanding changes in my own physical makeup that began in my early teens, it did not help with the intensity of feeling that comes with puberty, and what I'm about to tell you may lead you to think you are descended from a really neurotic kid.

I was interested in astronomy from the time my father told me, when I was five, how far away the moon was. (I remember him saying it was

238,000 miles away, and I was so flattered at being given a grown-up answer that it sparked an intense interest in related subjects.) I later learned of opposing forces called centrifugal and centripetal — and came to believe that the earth's orbit around the sun was a delicate balance between the tendency to fly off into outer space (centrifugal force) and the gravitational pull of the sun (centripetal force), and that the slightest disturbance would send it one way or the other.

We had an orchard on the farm I grew up on, and I once fell out of an apple tree I was climbing and hit the ground with painful force. What worried me was not whether I might have done myself some damage, but that jarring the earth that way might have destroyed the delicate balance that kept the earth in its orbit. I remember that in the next days I would go into a cornfield to the north of the house and watch the sun rise on these summer mornings and felt at one point that the sun seemed a little bigger each day than the day before. Sick with anxiety and regret, I believed the earth was going to spiral into the sun, and it was my fault. (A little knowledge is a dangerous thing.) I'm sure, had I gone to my father with this concern, he would have been able to reassure me that Gabriel was not about to blow his horn, but I was too frightened and ashamed and guilty to confess what I had done by falling out of that tree.

This is a tough stage of life, and you will probably have similar, though

not identical, problems before adulthood.

Adolescence

(10) **Adolescent.** Postpuberty pre-
dults are called adolescents,
and they are essentially grown
up, but not considered quite
adult, physically or in matters
of judgment. This is why they
are seldom governors, CEOs,
judges, presidents, or brain
surgeons. But adolescence is
an important and interesting
time of life, and should be respected for what it represents.

Humans have a lot of life that other
living things are denied. Many forms

of life go to seed at the end of their life cycle. By "going to seed" I mean developing genetic material to carry on to the next generation. These life-forms begin to produce seeds shortly before they die. Dandelions and salmon go to seed right at the end of their life. The yellow blossom of the weed dandelion turns white and becomes a ball of seeds with tiny white hairs that can dislodge themselves and float to other places. Salmon find their way back to where they were born and the males spawn by depositing their seed on fish eggs — and then they die.

Human beings are quite different: they go to seed as teenagers — that is, they produce sperm and eggs — and then they can live to one hundred or beyond, and enjoy all that extra life, working and playing and being parents, grandparents, great-grandparents, and in the case of your mother's mother's father's mother, Alma Mae Montee, the great-great-grandmother who knows you and enjoys your company.

Since everyone calls her Nana, I'm sure you will call her that, unless you make up something more suitable. You have elected (so your parents tell me) to call your father's mother Grandy (maybe you have mistaken her for a Spanish grandee), and Grandy's mother (who is Gam to your father) you are invited to call Great-gam, but I'll bet you'll think of something shorter. Languages don't provide words for concepts we don't have a lot of use for. Like numbers: a thousand million is a billion, and at each stage multiplying by a thousand, we have trillion, quadrillion, quintillion, sextillion, septillion, octillion, nonillion, and then what? There is no word for the number 10 taken to the power 31. It has no name. And all we can do with ancestors beyond grandparents is add the word "great" whatever number of times we need to go back into the past. To name a given ancestor back to the beginning of the Christian era (if such a person could be traced) you'd need about sixty "greats" before the word "grand." This is unwieldy.

Why am I rambling on like this? Probably because you are not refuting anything I have written, nor have you added anything, or derailed my train of thought by changing the subject. If reading this tends to put you to sleep, I trust you will merely go away from it for a while, and then come back again out of curiosity.

Adulthood

(11) **Young Adult.** When you have grown up you will be called and considered an adult. The good news is that now you are your own man, your own boss, and nobody can force you to do anything.

The bad news is the same thing. You are your own boss and since nobody can force you to do anything, you have the sole responsibility for your own actions and this burden is something new — and it may seem, at first, something heavy. You have the choice of conforming to certain social, cultural, and legal rules, or breaking them. If you have been taught well, you will realize that it is generally better to conform to these rules than to break them. If you find some laws are in diametric opposition to your conscience, you will seek to change them through your rights as a voter, and in extreme cases you may break these laws. People did this as a matter of conscience during the civil rights confrontations when laws stated that people of a different racial background must ride in the back of buses and drink out of different water fountains. Civil disobedience is a matter of choice, and I caution you to use it sparingly. But I will be proud of you if your principles and conscience move you to abandon obedience to immoral rules.

The remaining ages are (12) prime adulthood, (13) young middle age, (14) prime middle age, (15) young old age, (16) old old age, and (17) ancient. I'd like to deal with them in terms of decades of a life span.

But first I want to give you my idea of the chronological ages of each:

A young adult is	21–33
A prime adult is	34–55
A young middle-ager is	56–65
A prime middle-ager is	66–75
A young old person is	76–88
An old old person is	89–98
And an ancient is	99 and beyond.

Demographers and the compilers

of actuarial tables, in calculating life expectancies (the age that you have a fifty-fifty chance of reaching) do not let us have much time statistically beyond prime middle age, according to the categories I have laid out above, but when you consider the potential span (which is a little above 120 years), we are already asked to consider ourselves "old" forty-four years before the end of that potential life span, and "ancient" a full twenty-one years before.

Now to examine the twelve decades of human life: (And I wish them all on you, Xander. Granted, the odds are against either of us making it through the twelfth — it ends at age 120. It's a very slim chance, but it's always possible, because there have been humans who have made it.) If you take after me at all, you will never wish to live less than to the fullest. Go for the full *twelve* yards — 120 years. I never heard anyone 120 years old say he wished he had died at an earlier age. Perhaps one reason is I never met anyone 120 years old. But there's a chance you might meet such people. Find out how they feel at that age. (Of course, there's an outside chance you can ask me about that on my 120th birthday.) But that decade I have merely tacked on to the eleventh, since I know very little about it.

The longevity of your ancestors is said to be a potent factor in how long you will live. While there is truth in this, it is important to consider two factors in judging your own potential for long life: your ability to modify risks (health habits, caution and common sense, and access to preventive and corrective medicine), and knowledge of why a given ancestor had a shorter life than he should have had. Much of your ancestry comes from the American Midwest, and those who were transplanted from the British Isles, where there was iodine in the seafood they ate, found insufficient iodine in freshwater fish or crops of the field, and their thyroid glands suffered for this lack. Thyroid glands, desperately trying to trap any possible iodine in the area, will become enlarged, and form goiters. These are unsightly swellings that can interfere with breathing, and damage the heart. The Midwest came to be called the "goiter belt." Two of my (and your) ancestors died young (in their fifties and sixties) because of goiters — my mother and her father. By the time I was born, there was such a thing as iodized salt, and later frozen and even fresh ocean fish became available in the Midwest. A person killed by that kind of thyroid disorder might have lived to be very old if iodine had been a part of his or her diet.

First Decade:

Zero to Ten

We seem to give babies more early information about animals than about humans. Why is this? We teach them zoology before anthropology. Your room is already filled with stuffed animals: elephants, ducks, zebras, giraffes, frogs, and horses. There must be a reason for this. Are animals more trustworthy than humans? There are people who believe this. The American author and humorist Mark Twain once wrote, "If you take in a starving dog and make him prosperous, he will not bite you. This is the principle difference between a dog and a man." Animals can be trusted to behave as their particular species is obliged to behave. This doesn't mean you should trust a lion, if he is hungry, not to make a sandwich of you. Humans are more complicated. Sometimes they can be trusted. And it would seem somehow wrong to give a baby a stuffed human. A little later, dolls and action figures may come into play, but at the beginning it is simply animals.

From the time you were born up to the age of ten years, you will change more than any other decade of your life — more than all other decades combined. You will learn faster and more in any given minute or hour than in any other decade of your life. You will form tastes, beliefs, esthetic standards, and bases for judgment; you will establish ways of dealing with others and the physical world. You will have built a relationship with the universe that makes it *your* universe. While you will learn further facts and techniques in ensuing decades, your basic skills in learning and dealing with the total environment will be pretty well set by the time you are ten.

You may find your emotional landscape more interesting than commonly expected.

I remember being desperately in love when I was nine. It can happen. (Later I read Thomas Mann's story "Disorder and Early Sorrow" about a nine-year-old girl who was deeply in love, and I would have thought feelings of love in someone that young were nonsense if I hadn't experienced them.)

We lived in a double house, the other half of which was occupied by a family with two daughters, both older than I, but something triggered a romantic impulse in me for the younger of these girls, who played the piano. I could hear her late on summer evenings playing pieces like Edward MacDowell's "To a Wild Rose." Looking out my bedroom window I could see the stars, and the branches of a catalpa tree, from the seeds of which this girl had threaded a lei to put around my neck. The infatuation was so fierce I lost my appetite for a time and my parents were worried about me. The girl was part American Indian, having that hybrid beauty of Asiatic high cheekbones and a generous mouth. There was, on my part, no sexual component to this attraction that I was aware of, but the romantic attraction was powerful. It was so powerful it lasted almost two months! Then my appetite came back and I reverted to feeling as I had always felt about girls — that I would rather not be too close to them. Can you imagine? But I was nine. It was acutely embarrassing to be near a girl, even during the time I was in love.

I remember about a year later, when I was riding a school bus on which the only empty seat was between two girls, I chose to ride all the way home standing. I have no idea now why I felt that way, but I did until about one more year, and then it began to reverse itself — massively.

We moved to the farm when I was

ten and I entered what are commonly called the "formative years." Whether you will move to a farm at age ten is unknown to me, although I consider it rather unlikely. I doubt your life will be blighted by never living on a family farm, but since fate put me on one, there were pluses for me. You will find or make your own pluses wherever fate and your family set you down.

There is a substantial possibility that within this decade you will have one or more brothers or sisters. You will always be the oldest, but you might have trouble adjusting to the presence of that first one that follows you into the family, because you may have gotten used to being the star of the show, and the center of attention. Personal experience has led me to this conclusion. I am the oldest of three brothers, and when my brother Paul arrived I was not quite two. It was a traumatic experience for me, and not too pleasant for Paul either. I saw to that. I am told (although I do not remember this) that when he arrived and the family crowded around, aunts, uncles, a grandmother, and an older cousin — all making cooing sounds and speaking baby talk, and (more disgusting) paying no attention at all to me, I went to the little basket he was in, snatched off a knit bonnet he was wearing, threw it on the floor, and stomped on it. You may have more character than to do this kind of thing, but don't be surprised if it hurts a lot to find the spotlight suddenly aimed at another very young family member. You'll get used to it, and be the better for it.

Great-grandfather Bill Surles

Second Decade:
Ten to Twenty

I'm going to make an assumption here, and it is arbitrary but necessary and not unreasonable: I believe there is a better than even chance that humanity will avoid a nasty setback through nuclear miscalculation, pollution damage to the biosphere, or total economic collapse and widespread revolution. Granted, there is a chance that some combination of catastrophes could trigger a new Dark Age, resulting in circumstances for the world, or for our country, that

85

would make it difficult to have a quality life. But because a healthy mind awakes in the morning with the belief that it will not be destroyed today by a lightning bolt or a car crash, it will be assumed in this letter that you will have a life of reasonable longevity and on-balance happiness.

In other words, you should have a shot at living a life as basically happy and as long as mine, and mine, although punctuated and seasoned by the usual undesirable incidents, has been extremely happy.

In spite of some heavy events, I always seemed cushioned against trauma or shock. My uncle Malcolm died when I was thirteen, my one grandmother when I was seventeen, my remaining grandfather when I was twenty, the banks closed when I was eleven, Dad had a failed business when I was a junior in high school, and the Great Depression stamped out all frills for the family; but I do not remember any pall of gloom cast over us at any time, and we never went hungry. Part of the time we were able to eat because we had raised stock and crops on our small farm, and had barnyard fowl, patches of vegetables, and an orchard.

When the banks closed in 1932, my mother called my brothers and me in from play and said she had bad news: I thought maybe it was another death in the family, but she told us we probably would never see our money again. I remember that I had $11 in an account that I supposed they were going to make me buy school supplies with, and I couldn't have cared less. My brothers and I went outside and resumed our play.

As an adult, I have been fired; I have failed a lot of auditions in early broadcast jobs; I have had lumbar and cervical spine surgery, knee replacement, two kinds of eye surgery, and hospitalizations for a couple of systemic infections — one urinary tract infection and a weird disorder diagnosed as "Australian Woodside Throat" (don't ask me where I picked that up, never having been in Australia up to that point in my life). It is certainly true that "Life is what happens while we're busy making other plans." If I had known in advance of any of these impending miseries, I might have suffered some dread, but I didn't, and none of them was an ordeal. You will not escape troubles of this kind. But you will take them in stride, and your chances are good for as decent a life as I have been handed.

I hope your parents carry on what I consider a tradition in our line: answering all questions truthfully and adequately for the age at which they are asked. According to my parents, this started with them. Since they were both born in the Victorian era (prior to 1900), much about the physical aspects of life were simply not discussed with children (or for that matter, touched on by adults), and this produced a good deal of frigidity, guilt, and confusion among those trying to grow up and understand sex.

My father told me of an incident when he was a boy that illustrates the powerful taboos that darkened those times. His older brother had discovered a nest outside one of the basement windows where a hen was sitting on eggs. At the dinner table he asked if it was thought the eggs were fertile, pointing out the futility of trying to hatch eggs that were sterile. His mother picked up her plate of food and marched out of the room. You did not discuss such things in front of a Victorian lady, and my uncle was reprimanded for using a word like "fertile" in her presence.

It was at that time, my father said, that he promised himself he would not deal with the subject in such a cumbersome and ludicrous manner, and that any children he had would not be kept in ignorance about anything. He followed through on this, my mother agreeing wholeheartedly.

My brothers and I never felt ashamed to ask anything and never considered human sexuality to be a big deal — never any bigger than other important subjects, like economics or history. And your great-grandmother and I continued the tradition with our children, one of whom is your grandmother, and she continued it with her son, your father. (If you learn to read at an early age and you tackle this letter and are able to follow this philosophy and even this genealogy, I am prepared to congratulate you.) Please read it later, when you are older.

My parents taught me to read before I went to school, and when I started the first grade I was somewhat surprised that the other children were not reading. I remember showing off once by reading aloud to my parents from a newspaper. On encountering the word "futility" (the meaning and pronunciation of which I was ignorant) I forged ahead and spoke it, as I had been taught, phonetically, and it came out "fuh-tel-*itty*" — and I wondered why they laughed at me.

This decade (your second, ages ten to twenty) spans 2012 to 2022 and will be dented by unhappy world events, I fear: the easy access of high-tech weaponry to fanatic groups will continue to plague civilization, and this is something I don't expect to be put under control while you are a teenager. Terrorism and brushfire wars may be the price we pay for not lobbing thermonuclear bombs at one another. (One theory: the human will to survive is strong enough to prevent nuclear holocaust, but the aggression we can't curb will come out in other ways.) There may be significance in the fact that every weapon devised by man has been used in anger within the past five years — *except* the hydrogen bomb. We've had it for over a half century and not used it — yet. I like to think this is because the will to survive is greater than narrow national interests, and we will, at all costs, avoid an exchange that would make the planet uninhabitable by mammals. (Cockroaches might survive and inherit the earth, but not humans.) I do think the economy will have improved from the condition it was in when you were born, but the problems that depressed it will not have been solved.

Changing from Child to Adult

You will change a great deal in these years from ten to twenty — physically, mentally, emotionally, and in the matter of independence. While they come on gradually, the changes are profound: increase of body size and musculature, the appearance of secondary sex characteristics, changes in the circulatory and endocrine systems, the appearance of real earning power, acceptance in the community as an adult — all these are more or less inevitable. Some are bewildering, but many are sources of immense satisfaction. You will be keenly aware that you are becoming your own person and this is a great feeling!

You will, I assume, graduate from

high school and go on to college. Academic credentials are passports not only to professional success, but, if they are the right ones — if you have gotten an education and not just training — they can lead you to enhanced enjoyment of living.

Consider again how fortunate you are: fewer than one percent of humans on this planet get a college education. One percent! You will probably want to give back some of your good fortune in some way, and that too is a source of enjoyment of life.

I have no desire to try to instruct you in what my parents' generation called "The birds and the bees" — you'd probably be ahead of me anyway, but knowing that it's in this second decade of life you will mature sexually, and start the process of establishing relationships, and experiencing the whole range of emotional and physical feelings that go with the territory — the sick, neurotic beauty of infatuation; the mangling anguish of rejection; the anxious embarrassment of trying to reverse an unrequited affection; the ecstasy of orgasm; and possibly, eventually, the unsurpassed joy of loving someone deeply who loves you in return — physically, emotionally, intellectually, and spiritually — knowing it's in these ten years that this will start coming down on you, I feel I ought to share some experience and outlook that might be useful to you. Being lucky in love can be helped by some effort, and you've got a good shot at it.

You will probably produce children, although that's a matter of personal choice. You will likely be heterosexual, but there is a small chance you could be gay. And if you are of that persuasion I would feel concern for you. But only for one reason: the society we are embedded in right now is not up to handling sexuality with much maturity or understanding. Our hang-ups are not as severe as those of the Victorians or of some repressive religious cultures. But even though you would be just as worthy a person, life might be a tougher row to hoe if you were to be gay. And this would sadden me.

My personal odyssey of getting all the blocks into an order that spelled something is mildly amusing and possibly instructive. I already mentioned my meltdown at age nine over (literally) the girl next door. Even though I have nothing left of that feeling for her, I can remember the intensity of it and still see her face vividly in memory. Between that and my next significant encounter there was little you would find edifying about my amorous development.

But nine years later I found myself mired in a mutual attraction that was physical, and little more. This with a girl six years older than I, who was explosively voluptuous, and who somehow thought I was as attractive as I thought she was, and managed to mask her nymphomania to a point of respectability. She actually wanted me to believe she was a virgin. I, on the other hand, wanted her to believe I was a man of the world who had vast experience in this department. I did not for a minute believe she was a virgin, and she must have known it was my first time, but we played out our little scene with courtesy and compassion, each respecting the other's lie.

So now I had experienced love without sex and sex without love. I began to wonder if the two were ever brought together. Our torrid and temporary affair took place mostly in a car. Her car — I didn't own one. (Automotive sex was very big in that day. Car designers today are either less talented, or they are prudes. Bucket seats and midbench armrests do not provide a hospitable or inviting atmosphere for dalliance.) Her name is unimportant to you or anyone else reading this, and she may still be living, so I will draw the curtain on this scene.

I had yet to experience at the same time a combination of love and sex from an adored partner who reciprocated my ardor, but I can tell you that when that comes about, and I hope it will for you, it is not additive, it is exponential. This "terrible beauty in armor," as Stephen Vincent Benét called it, is at the summit of human experience. A powerfully romantic link, adorned with trust, adoration, spiritual rapport, and comradeship, at a sexual coupling that mingles almost every body fluid — sweat, saliva, snot, tears, semen — is a connection that reaches the highest ground of human intimacy, makes it as though nothing you have ever been or done before had any color or reality to it. It is not exaggeration to say that this is what life is all about. Life can hand you many satisfactions: you can attain achievement in sports, art, business, writing, philanthropy, science, etc.; and you can have a good life with commitments and accomplishments and the rewards of achieving. But your life will be in black-and-white unless you are lucky enough to experience real love.

So much about the subject has become cliché. It has become cliché because it is so often said. And it is so often said because it is *true.* I wish it for you, Xander.

Great-grandmother Peggy Surles

Third Decade:

Twenty to Thirty

After one year in this decade you become a young adult. Just why twenty-one is a milestone in marking maturity is not clear to me. Why not twenty?

One of the changes taking place at this point in your life is in your father, who has been an idiot since you were about seventeen. He suddenly becomes wise again, within half a dozen years, and appears to have the potential of becoming a good friend.

In the early years (twenty to

twenty-four) there is an opportunity to tone down excesses and establish habits that can make you feel better and preserve your health. If you are maturing at a decent rate, you will weary of partying and a lot of boisterous activities that seemed important in your teens. Not everybody does. There are people who get stuck in this phase of life and carry it into middle years — in some cases into advanced years. They usually do not have a pretty life, although the importance of making it appear so remains high.

When I was fifteen I used to get up just about every morning feeling so good I didn't think I deserved it. I would stride forth into the day with animal energy and an emotional state bordering on euphoria. By the time I was twenty-five, I felt bad most of the time. If I had to get out of bed early, I did so grudgingly and with a headache. I did not anticipate obligatory chores with any joy. What was so obtuse about my mental processes then was that I did not realize right away what had brought about this sad change in me. I thought it was the normal adult-human condition to feel bad when you were twenty-five. And I remembered what it was like to be fifteen.

I am somewhat ashamed to say that it took me a while to understand what was going on. When I was fifteen my habits were, if not exemplary, at least a lot healthier. When I was twenty-five I was smoking two-plus packs of cigarettes every day, drinking alcohol in quantities not designed to protect the liver, getting less sleep than recommended, and following a pattern of nutrition that would have starved and poisoned self-respecting swine. It was not the normal adult situation: it was a case of bad habits carried into my mid-twenties.

If anyone had told me back then that I could feel as good again as I did at age fifteen, and that I could carry most of that feeling into my fifties, sixties, seventies, and eighties, I would have dismissed the idea as ridiculous. But it is true. Once I cleaned up my act I felt good again.

I pass this on to you in case you fall into bad habits and are puzzled by their effects. You may, of course, never fall into this trap. You may be like your father. At no point in his life did he feel peer pressure of any kind.

In fact, he exerted peer pressure. His mother once said, "If he falls in with bad company, he'll get them straightened out." And I saw an example of this. He had a friend when he was in high school who was a dissolute sort, and his grandmother and I were naturally concerned about the friendship. But the influence went the other way: he got his friend to cut down on his drinking and steered him around a temptation to experiment with drugs. Your dad is one who sets fashion rather than follows it.

A person's third decade is a powerful one. And it takes a long time to unfold. (Not as long as the first ten years of life, because that decade seems like eternity, and the second ten years is tumultuous, with all the physical and emotional changes.) But in my memory, the decade between 1941 and 1951 (my third — that is, ages twenty to thirty) took about thirty-five years to run out — whereas the decade between 1991 and 2001 (my eighth) went by in maybe fourteen months. People are always saying that the older you get, the faster time goes. But I don't see it that way. Time does not seem to pass faster the older you get — *it seems to have passed faster.* It's in looking back that it whizzed by so fast.

It's in our twenties that we begin to get hints of what earlier experiences may have contributed to the attitudes, reactions, and perspectives of our adult existence. (I came to Chicago in my early twenties to take a job with the National Broadcasting Company in its Central Division.) I have to back up to when I was six years old and going to the Horace Mann School in Lima. A classmate of mine in the second grade, Herbert Oyer (who retired recently from a brilliant medical career as an expert on hearing), had an older brother who used to help me with my roller skates. I never could work the key to clamp them properly onto my shoes. One day Herbert's brother told me his family was going to move to Chicago. I had to ask what a Chicago was. He said, "That's where the gangsters are." So I had to ask what gangsters were. He said, "They kill people." And I remember thinking, Why on earth would the Oyer family want to move to someplace where they kill people?

They moved to Chicago, and six

weeks later, my parents told me that Herbert's father had been killed in a jewelry store robbery. He just happened to be there at the wrong time. I was sad for the family, but not surprised, because that's where the gangsters were! Sixteen years later, when I entered the city of Chicago for the first time, uppermost in my mind was the question, Is this a prudent move? Should I be locating here where I will probably be killed by a gangster? So you see how early experiences can mold your outlook — your fears, hopes, the whole way you view the world.

In the third decade you will likely wrap up your formal education. You may not. You're never too old to learn. You may marry and start a family. You have a chance of enjoying some career advances and triumphs, you begin to see an ebb of uncertainty about the future, and at the same time you run risks, ranging from accident and illness to possible financial reverses and the temporary insanity testosterone can cause in an otherwise sensible male. Beware of this.

My own third decade had so much happening in it I look back and marvel at the circumstances and my relatively lighthearted reaction to the constantly shifting landscape. In that one decade I moved up from being a staff announcer at a radio station in my hometown to the position of program director, went to Detroit to join the staff of WWJ radio there, enrolled in Wayne University (now Wayne State), went into the army after Pearl

Harbor was attacked, met and became engaged to my life partner, a girl I met in Chicago who is now your great-grandmother, married, had two children, began my television career, and became part of the two major programs feeding the NBC network from Chicago — a puppet show called *Kukla, Fran and Ollie* and the soap opera *Hawkins Falls*. My income was increased in that period by 600 percent, and I published my first book. I also had a throat operation during which I nearly bled to death. (You apparently did not inherit my bleeding tendencies and I am happy about that — and happy also that in my later years I have more or less outgrown that disorder.) I also made the shift from radio to TV, bought a car, and moved to the suburbs after buying a house. That was a decade crowded with events — much more so than later ones.

It was also in this decade (I was twenty-three) that I first saw the St. John's Booklist — the famous curriculum that comprised the great books (later renamed the Great Books of the Western World). I was so ashamed of how few of them I had read (there were 131 in that original list, compiled by Scott Buchanan and Stringfellow Barr) that I made up my mind to read them all. I planned to do this in seven years. I reasoned that seven years after the time I decided to do this, I would be seven years older, even if I had read *nothing*.

It took me thirteen years to read them all. But I finished (after opening up the list to read other things) in

1957, when I was thirty-six — and it had a curious effect on my life later (in the eighth decade), which I will tell you about farther on.

You will have chosen your profession early in this ten-year period, or fate will have chosen it for you. A word about life work. Whoever said, "Find pleasure in your work or you will not find pleasure" was not a Puritan. The Puritan view was that you should be suspicious of enjoying anything, even your duties. Drudge your way through life, and you would be rewarded in the next life. The devil was in everything pleasurable. While it is true that you should enjoy what you do for a living if living is to be worthwhile, there are pleasures outside of how you make money. Our culture tends to identify people by how they make their living. Not so in all cultures. In Switzerland you might ask a young man what he does and he might reply, "I write poetry," or "I climb mountains." He may be a bank teller or construction worker, but what he *does* is, in his mind, what makes his life worthwhile, not how he earns his keep.

Second, you may have more than one profession. Recent times have seen an increase in adult education, and job and career changes, made possible by the longer life expectancy. This will free you from the demand that you identify yourself through your job. In twentieth-century America, if a Leonardo da Vinci had appeared in our midst he would not have been recognized, because he would have had to choose one line of work — he would have had to declare himself a painter, sculptor, engineer, poet, writer, whatever — and then everything else he did would have been considered interesting hobbies. I think that is changing. If you want to be several things, you can.

Several years ago your great-uncle and my son Hugh R. Downs wrote an article titled "The Disappearance of Computers." When H.R. showed it to me I said, "You don't really think computers are going to disappear, do you?" And he said, "They're not going to cease to exist, but they are going to disappear. The time is coming when the keyboard and the monitor and the mouse will be as quaint as a typewriter. They will all be supersmart chips in our cars, our clothing, our paper, walls, tables, appliances, jewelry, and in some cases implanted into our bodies." This was prophetic. It's happening.

More important than the changes in technology are potential changes in the way you see things. The most profound change I underwent toward the end of my third decade (when I was almost thirty) came from reading about Stoicism. I read the *Encheiridion* of Epictetus, and the Emperor Marcus Aurelius's *Meditations*. I had thought vaguely of Stoicism as something that meant you didn't cry out if you were in pain. But I found it something very different, and it taught me three important things:

(1) That I didn't have to hate anybody. I had some hatreds,

but learned that you only hate what you fear, and if you can come to realize you don't have to fear anyone, you will no longer hate anyone.

(2) That you should not concern yourself with anything not in your power to change. I thought this a tall order, but a little practice gave me a useful method of ignoring such things.

This is what happened: I had been cutting it close, getting to work on time. If I didn't leave the house early enough for a comfortable margin in making the trip to the studios, I would sit on the elevated train urging it forward faster with body English, and cursing the passengers who got on and off at stops too slowly for my tight schedule, and getting to my destination an irritable, nervous wreck. But I finally separated out what was in my power to control. I could leave a little earlier. How fast I walked to the train station was in my power. How fast I walked away from the train at the Merchandise Mart and toward the studios was in my power. But the speed of the train was not in my power.

I finally got so I could focus on my pace to the station, and then once aboard a train, take out a book or newspaper and lay down the burden of worry about whether I would be on time, and then on arrival pick up the burden again and hasten, if necessary, to the NBC studios. In time I could apply this to other situations.

(3) I learned that to adopt a useful philosophy you should not mount an assault on the summit, but should move there one step at a time. Try a little bit, and when results are forthcoming, try the next step. Corny, but it works.

On your thirtieth birthday anniversary you will glide into decade four.

Great-grandfather Hugh Downs (Poppy)

Fourth Decade:

Thirty to Forty

About midway into this ten-year stretch you become a prime adult. You will plateau for several years, at the height of your powers. As some of them begin to wane, others will increase in intensity. For example, your physical prowess will decline (slightly) from an athletic standpoint, but your experiences will accumulate, allowing you to hone techniques for dealing with decremental changes, including the emotional concern about those changes — so that you can stay on the crest of your prime in and through the sixth decade. In this one you can begin to translate knowledge into wisdom.

It's also in this decade that you might suffer a diminution of esthetic appreciation and romance. If this happens, it is probably because life has a habit of pounding us into submission, so that we feel obliged to focus on the practical aspects of living — to the point that we lose sight of our original goals of quality living: zest, mild obsession, romance, and maintenance of a hierarchy of values. It may be more complicated than that. But I know from experience that after I had suffered some decline in enjoying things I considered beautiful, and lost a little zest and some of the romance my marriage had sustained for almost a score of years — I thought (again) that this was the normal course of events as one got older.

I was dead wrong. It all began to come back in my late fifties, and I'll tell you more about that later. (It had much to do with having an understanding wife.)

Broadcasting helped me enormously in keeping life challenging and fresh. Even when the keenness of my general interest in things began to wane, I would find some specific topic or adventure that rekindled my ability to flavor a project with some youthful feelings. On some subjects I may have started with tepid interest, but on getting into them, would develop a keen sense of curiosity and then a desire to explore. And it was hard for me to pass up a chance to learn a skill.

High-visibility professions can bring some marvelous perks, and some dangers and annoyances, but on balance, broadcasting has enhanced my life enormously. First of all, I have enjoyed it from the start. I have done things and been involved in projects I could not have bought my way into if I were a billionaire. I will share some of these with you, because of what they did for me in terms of perspective and insight, and how they shaped my attitudes and sense of security and overall philosophy.

One such project was this: When I was thirty-four I put together a segment on scuba diving for an NBC program that involved showing what steps to take to learn diving. In those days (1955) there was no certification. You could buy a tank and regulator and go out and drown yourself. Many did. As a result, small groups of divers decided to structure some kind of guidelines. Organizations were formed, with these guidelines for safety and courtesy, and the sport became a lot safer. But long before I was certified I had lessons from an equipment manufacturer's representative, and learned scuba in the pool at the Beverly Hilton Hotel in Beverly Hills, California. It had been heated close to body temperature to show an act called "water babies." It may seem hard to believe, but the people running this act would fling newborn babies into the water to demonstrate that fear of water is learned at a later age. These infants would float around underwater with their eyes open, and they would not inhale the water or panic in any way. The theory was that since you spend the first nine months of your existence in amniotic fluid inside your mother, you are used to being underwater. Another facet of the theory is that fear of water is learned — probably from hearing grown-ups tell you in frightened voices never to go near the water because you can drown. The theory may be true but I don't recommend throwing the very young into the drink. It may prove something, but I can't see any plus in it for the babies.

But we broadcast this, plus a female diving team — not scuba diving but diving off boards of various heights. The girls were skilled and scenic. One of them lost a contact lens in the pool and I volunteered to look for it. (Naturally, I wanted to put my newfound skill to some practical use.) The task was worse than looking for a needle in a haystack. The index of refraction of a contact lens is just about identical to that of water, so the lens was completely invisible. I felt around the bottom of the pool, fruitlessly. But the project gave me a strange experience: I had a full tank of air and weights enough that I didn't have to struggle to stay down. After twenty or twenty-five minutes I concluded the lens must have gone down the deep-end drain, but I was sleepy, and I lay there on the bottom resting, and in a short time I went sound asleep. What woke me was a metallic sound from each breath as the tank ran low on air. (There was a reserve rod on the side of the tank that you could pull when the tank ran out, and it would give you three minutes or so more breathing time. This is all obsolete technology now.) But as I lay there, semifloating and in something of a fetal position, I had a strange dream, unlike any I'd had before or have had since. I imagined myself to be floating in space beside a large body like the moon, but the horizon of it was vertical, so I was drifting beside it in the void of empty space. When I came to, I had a moment of not wanting to wake up because of how beautiful this all seemed to me, and there was an internal debate over whether I should rouse myself and do anything about my situation, or just drift away forever. Gradually I realized where I was, and what was going on, and I came to the surface.

There was no one with me in the pool. (To my knowledge even the buddy system of pairs of divers was not yet in place in the diving world. And that has since been abandoned, since it's a lot safer to have extra regulators to give people in distress, rather than share your own with someone who may, in a panic, glom on to it and not give it back to you.) At that time, my instructor did not caution me about not holding my breath on ascent. Even a few feet up to the surface holding a full breath from a regulator can stretch the lungs painfully. And a full breath at ambient pressure at real depth (more than fifteen feet) can be fatal, tearing the lungs and causing you to drown in your own blood. Years later when I taught diving, the first thing I stressed to a student was not to hold his breath when rising. Keep breathing. Some people had gathered to watch the start of my search for the missing contact lens, but they had got bored and went away. I got bored and went to sleep!

Burdens of Being a Prime Adult

You may find yourself a member of what was once called the "sandwich generation." In addition to the business of making a living and guiding a career, you have responsibility for your children and a concern for aging parents. Probably a good thing you are a prime adult, because you are right in the middle, and can be called on for a lot.

But you have lovely margins. One of the differences between youth and age — even midlife and age — is that the margins get thinner as you get older. When young you can be profligate of your energies, or mildly abusive to your system: you are carving into margins that are fat. I once interviewed a man who was eighty-five on the old *Today* show. After he said his age, I asked him, "How do you feel?" He said, "I feel fine. In fact I feel like I did when I was thirty-five — as long as I don't *do* what I did when I was thirty-five!"

If you have to lose a night's sleep it won't bend you any. I can remember going two consecutive nights without sleep. I don't recommend it — at any age. I felt like there was a rock in my chest.

I did not have the burden of caring for aging parents. Tragically, my mother died when I was thirty-seven. She was never an invalid, but a thyroid condition had damaged her heart. As I told you earlier, she was of that transplanted English stock that did not have access to food from the sea or iodized salt, and lived in the so-called goiter belt. She was only sixty-eight. My father lived alone for a while and then married a woman who had been a friend of my mother's, and of whom I heard my mother say, "If anything ever happens to me, I hope you'll marry Mary Louise." And he did. They were married for thirteen years, and he lost her. So he was widowed twice. He said something to me that tore me up: "I can tell you that it isn't any easier the second time." Dad lived to be almost eighty-four, but he, too, was never an invalid.

This letter has a stream-of-consciousness format that I ask you to forgive, but rambling on is something I majored in in college. Among random memories of my father is one just before I turned thirty-one. He was visiting us, and your grandmother Deirdre was not quite three. Shortly after a Sunday dinner, when the table had been cleared and nearly everyone had left, I came on the following scene: Dad was trying to take a nap on the floor, and Deirdre was standing on his stomach, saying, "Guess where I am, Grandpa!"

Does this sound like proper behavior for your grandmother to display?

Puncturing the dignity of ancestors is a favorite human pastime, for some perverse reason. I remember an incident involving Dad from sixty-nine years ago. (Maybe you had to be there to understand how funny it was, but you will have your own stories as your life unfolds. It wasn't really funny to Dad.)

We were living on the farm. I was twelve, Paul was ten, and Wally was six. Dad had felled a dead but fairly large tree to the west of the chicken house, and had cut up the trunk and branches for firewood. He had a lot of brush left over, which he burned. In preparing to burn it he built a pyre that was the size of a large igloo, but decided right after lighting it at the base on the windward side that it was too loosely piled. So he mounted this hill of brush and started jumping on it to tamp it down a bit. Dad at this time weighed close to 230 pounds, and silhouetted against the sky he gave the appearance of a giant anthropoid ape venting his rage. My brother Paul and I were not needed for this operation and were simply spectators. As the fire took hold and Dad continued to tamp down his mound of boughs and twigs, his foot went into a hole and he lost his balance, rolling down toward the fire and pulling a lot of brush in on top of him.

To our infinite discredit, Paul and I were laughing too hard to be of help to him. Wally was confined to the house, suffering from a bad cold, but he was standing at the window watching this tableau and all we could see of his face was the inside of his mouth. He was laughing as hard as we were. Dad escaped unharmed, but for a moment I did not think my brothers and I would. Paul and I hid out in the barn.

The Security Issue Again

Around this age you may find something to anchor your life to, so your sense of security is healthy. (It may be healthy without anchoring to anything, but in a world that can seem like hastily sliding plate tectonics or shifting sands, some people feel better with an anchor if they can find it.) For some, this may be one person to trust and love: for others it is a set of principles, or a religion, or a cause, or dedication to integrity, or a scientific theory, or devotion to humanity. These are not all equally dependable. Human beings can leave you or die, and today's orthodox scientific theory can wind up in tomorrow's dustbin. Setting your anchor in the foul ground of pure expediency and self-aggrandizement is a valueless exercise. (It's amazing how many people do this, though.)

This may, of course, be something you have acted on earlier, or something you won't concern yourself with until later years, or never. But it's worth a thought. Religion appears to have more permanence. Historian Will Durant referred to the "indestructible piety of mankind." You might attach yourself to some organized sect, or you may, like Thomas Carlyle, find that "There is one True

Church, of which at present I am the only member."

In Tolstoy's *War and Peace*, Prince Andrew, who dies of battle wounds, in his last thoughts saw love as the substrate of everything. " 'What is love?' he thought. 'Love hinders death. Love is life. All, everything that I understand I understand only because I love. Everything is united by it alone. Love is God, and to die means that I, a particle of love, shall return to the general and eternal source.' "

Everyone who has ever been in love knows how it colors and affects everything else. I suppose that is something one could consider an anchor. The love of a single individual can have an eternal quality — an unchanging reality, even after death.

The philosopher John Stuart Mill said of his dead wife, "Her memory is like a religion to me."

Religion and politics are two things you're not supposed to bring up in polite conversation. So I'll bring up politics right now and religion a few chapters later. (This is not a conversation, polite or not, since right now, at age three months, you insist on words that are your own, and don't appear to understand my language. And you will learn mine before I learn yours. While I'm digressing, can you tell me what some of your words mean? Sometimes in a talkative mood, you have such an earnest look on your face. You are trying to get me to understand something you want to get across. What does "aura-bag" mean? Or "gleer"? Or once with a shake of your head you said "moisbiss" and followed it with a stare that showed astonishment that I couldn't understand. My ignorance is causing you to cast pearls before my snout and waste a great deal of valuable insights on the desert air. Give me time. In a few more months I am sure we'll have a common language.)

Politics is a rough business. A statesman has to be a politician, but has to be a principled politician, which is considered an oxymoron. However, there are such people, rare as they may be. A person goes into politics for one of two reasons: either he relishes power and the prospect of personal wealth once out of office, or he really believes that the community has a need that he is best suited to serve. Grieve for the politico who is thin-skinned, private, and sensitive, and unaware of public fickleness and cruelty. Harry Truman said, "If you can't stand the heat, stay out of the kitchen."

There are two reasons I never sought public office. One, I never felt I was the best person for any given office from a public welfare standpoint, and two, since I have spent my career life in mass media in an attempt to ingratiate myself with the whole broadcast audience, and know that to run for office on the ticket of a political party is to alienate half the public at one stroke and a lot of the other half later on, I could see nothing in it for me or for the community.

So you'll be forty years old at the

end of this decade. Your circumstances are unknown to me in this veiled future. It will be 2042, and the only thing I know is the world will be very different.

I try to envision it: you will probably enjoy the individual customization of every manufactured item you buy. This will give merchandise a flavor once again of those cottage industries prior to mass production. Assembly lines will still exist but through computer programming, just about everything will be unique.

Electronic appliances wired together may be museum material by now. Wireless personal communication had a start before you were born, and must now be the rule rather than the exception. The air will be filled with raw and encrypted information, and ever smaller wireless units will be processing googleplex gigabytes of information, some of them even useful.

I like to think that using animals to test drugs and medical procedures will be a thing of the past — replaced by computer models. Even drug tests on humans will have been taken over by biochemical simulators. Ray Kurzweil believes that telephone communication will be able to throw up life-size holographic images of the person called in three-dimensional, full-color action and believability. (This aspect of virtual reality may prove troublesome. We have enough of a problem with *real* reality without having to cope with the virtual kind. And the holographic life-size image of a girl you call and pull out of the shower may prove more stimulating than you can cope with.)

I can only begin to imagine the automotive world on your fortieth birthday. It will probably be a lot safer in terms of fatalities per passenger mile, and the cars will talk to you more and coddle you and do much of your work for you. They may also be faster, but it's hard to imagine why that is needed. There may be other impressive transport changes: the space plane could be a reality, following a suborbital trajectory from New York to Tokyo in three hours or so (I'm guessing) but with not enough speed to endanger the hull with excessive heat on reentry. And I believe there will be tourists in space — at least out to a low-orbit platform like the space station. Mars may be for another generation.

Four great-grandparents: Norman and Barbara
Montee, Ruth and Hugh Downs,
and a very young you

Fifth Decade:

Forty to Fifty

Before this ten years is over, Xander, you will have run through the first half of the new century. (It doesn't take long to demolish a century, I have found. I have now lived in all four quarters of the twentieth century and one of the twenty-first.)

You are still prime. If there is now in the world some control of viral infections, and new forms of dangerous microbes have been held at bay, most remaining diseases will be degenerative, so that means a statistical increase in diseases not caused by bacteria, viruses, or prions. But by staving off the onset of degenerative disorders, which I imagine medical science will have got a handle on by now, you and your cohorts should be enjoying much greater life expectancy. I am guessing that before you are fifty, life expectancy will be eighty-three for men and eighty-four for women. Contrast that with expectancy at the time I'm writing this — seventy-four for men and seventy-eight for women. (The gap between men and women will have narrowed because female lifestyles may be more similar to male's.) Or contrast it with life expectancy at the time Queen Victoria died (1901): about forty-nine for both men and women.

And we not only live longer; we live

more per day, week, year, than previous generations. My grandfather Sherman Downs lived his life in Ohio within a short radius of his farm in Champaign County. He made one trip to Kansas and one to New York — the latter during WWI. His oldest son, my uncle Malcolm, was ill with influenza in an army hospital, and they thought he was going to die. (He didn't but many did, from that flu epidemic.) The provincial nature of life in the rural Midwest back then is shown up in a story (possibly apocryphal) that I heard when I was little. When my grandfather got back from the New York trip, a neighbor is reported to have said to him, "Been to New York, eh, Sherm?" Gramp said yes. The neighbor asked, "Who runs the hotel there now?"

I contrast my grandfather's travels with my own. By the mid-sixties I had lost track of how many times I had flown from one coast to the other. As members of the Circumnavigators' Club, your great-grandmother and I were asked how many times we had been around the world. It was either four or five, but we couldn't be sure. Several times we have been to the other side of the planet and come home by continuing in the same direction — circling the globe. But on one trip we really can't remember whether we came back the way we had gone or continued on around!

The amount of information we process with all the media and available entertainments we have is many times that of nineteenth-century citizens. So we crowd more life into our years, and have more years than they did.

A high point of my life was being asked to serve on an advisory panel (a "committee of consultants") for over-hauling Britannica's Great Books of the Western World. There were seventeen of us. Historian Daniel Bell, Stephen Jay Gould, Father Theodore Hesburgh, Bill Moyers, and Martin E. Marty were among the panelists. I had been asked because once, in a room full of scholars at the Center for the Study of Democratic Institutions in Santa Barbara, California, Robert Hutchins and I were found to be the only ones who had read all of the great books. Britannica was apparently impressed by this and asked me to be part of the group that helped revise the list.

I would imagine that by this point in your life there will be more attention paid to water than to oil. As oil reserves dwindle and become more costly to recover, industrialized nations will have been forced to mount serious research into the development of alternative energy sources: wind and tide, thermal gradient, solar, and hell-power (tapping the magma that produces volcanoes). Your automobiles will probably be powered by fuel cells or the equivalent, each wheel driven by electric motors. The exhaust will be pure water. There may be cars powered by burning hydrogen directly, but since it requires energy to liberate the hydrogen from compounds it's bound up in (mostly water), these alternative sources will be called on for a great deal of energy, even if the world population will have stopped increasing by this time.

The overall need for oil may have declined, the whole petroleum industry withering much as whale oil retreated into history when petroleum replaced it. With the alternative sources available worldwide, international tensions created by the concentration of large oil reserves in the Middle East may be reduced. And of course, if petroleum won't be needed as a primary source of energy, it will still be the source of plastics, and these are so much a part of our lives that unless we have come up with an ability to synthesize hydrocarbon compounds that mimic petroleum, we may still be, to a certain extent, dependent on oil.

By now you will have already seen a move to a nonpolluting economy and possibly some decrease in the rampant population growth that has been going on since the dawn of the Industrial Revolution. I base this conjecture on a trend in the early twenty-first century: population is still increasing, but the explosive *rate* of increase is decreasing. China has made some inroads on its runaway population increase, and we are looking to India to follow suit. Of course, if there is a large war, there may be delays on all this. History sees human advance as two steps ahead and a big step back. If a war were large enough, it could, of course, result in a *decrease* in population.

I hope, in reviewing your life up to now, you are enjoying various evidences of success. And that in assessing your own advancement, you set your expectations high, but not too high. This is the time of life — the middle of your prime years — when you will begin thinking about whether you have made of your life what you wanted it to be. Are you happy in your present circumstances? Do situations that need correcting appear correctable? Are your goals for the future of a kind that are reasonably attainable? Around age forty-five you can stumble into what some have termed a midlife crisis. "How successful, *really*," you ask yourself, "is my career, marriage, potential for happiness, etc.?"

Goals can be appropriately lofty, if you have fallback positions in place. It may be all right to aspire to the presidency of the United States even though the chances of getting there are slim. (It is a reasonable goal, since men from unlikely backgrounds have been president.) However, if you're not going to be happy unless you become monarch of the entire unified globe, you are doomed to unhappiness. And however realistic the goals you set, you will be wise to have some of these fallback positions you're willing to settle for, in case you are absolutely blocked from your primary target.

Some years ago I did a feature for my TV program *20/20* on a twenty-fifth-anniversary reunion of Harvard graduates. In it I interviewed several of them to show a variety of attitudes and opinions about having graduated from Harvard and where it had led them, and how they felt about it. They were forty-six years old.

Among those selected for interviews, we found two who formed a remarkable contrast. The first one was a garage mechanic, who liked cars, apparently didn't feel he needed a large income, and believed his education had enhanced his appreciation of life in cultural and analytical matters. He enjoyed movies and spectator sports, and was happy with his wife and teenage daughter. He struck me as a well-adjusted person.

The other one had published a couple of books, had garnered some respect for his expertise about a social issue that comprised his Ph.D. thesis. But he was bitterly disappointed that he had not done better. Apparently he felt a Harvard diploma and a doctorate from that great university should have carried him to enormous heights — should have allowed him to set the world on fire. And in his mind he had failed. I was sad for him.

Success is a matter of adjustment. If you achieve what you set out to achieve, you will be successful, if the goal had value from the start. If you fall short of a goal, but realize along the way that there are other valuable goals, and are flexible enough to shift to better ones, you will also be successful. If the values you cherish have evolved only from the short-term, the selfish, the hedonistic, the frivolous — your success will not be genuine. Values that allow and encourage commitment and the desire to contribute to others, produce some enlightenment, and ratchet the community one notch higher in quality of life are the ones that will undergird success of the kind you want. It's all right if this is in part motivated by a desire to be thought of as a noble person. Vanity is not detrimental unless it is given top priority.

At this stage of your life not everything you do must be judged by how noble it is. You will give way to some frivolous impulses, which are not immediately explicable — maybe not ever. And it won't mean you are a bad guy. I am saying this because I need to believe that some of my actions were okay, even though it is hard to find anything socially redeeming about them. (They were not my life goals, however.) One I want to share with you, because I think I have finally figured out why I did what I did.

Early in the fifth decade of my life I received a Father's Day gift from my children and my wife. It was a sextant — an instrument for accurately measuring how far above the horizon the sun, moon, or any of the forty-some navigation stars are. This, along with a dependable clock, will allow you to know where you are on the surface of the earth, even when you are in the middle of an ocean. They knew of my interest in astronomy, and that navigation intrigues me. Sailing also intrigues me. I thought it was a hell of a gift.

In the next few years I planned a trip across the Pacific. I was obsessed with the idea of navigating my way across that vast stretch of sea. I finally set a date on which I wanted to leave. After studying the Hydrographic Office's sailing directions, I knew the best time of year to tackle those latitudes, and decided I would leave from Fort Lauderdale, Florida, around the end of June, and after coming through the Panama Canal would be entering the Pacific when it was most pacific, and hopefully would arrive in French Polynesia before the weather roughened. This was 1961. I decided to leave in late June 1965.

In the next four years I taught myself navigation by reading Bowditch and Weems and Dutton and Mixter on the subject, and later consulted Tom Nicholson of the Hayden Planetarium (who taught navigation at the Merchant Marine Academy). One vacation I arranged to do some out-of-sight-of-land navigating west of the Windward and Leeward Islands to see if I could make a proper landfall. It really worked!

I wanted my son with me, and he was available. He would be nineteen when we left. (Hugh Raymond Downs, your great-uncle on your father's side, is a remarkable man. You will enjoy meeting him when you are old enough. He has multiple talents and a great sense of humor.) I wanted six hands for deck duty and a professional cook for this voyage. (I had done just enough cooking at sea to know what an odious job it is.) All the rest would be what they call "Corinthian" crew — amateurs. The company comprised Pete Jackson, brother of the man I chartered the boat from; Bob Dixon, a young mechanic from Florida; Jerry Galyean, a young cinematographer; and Virgil Bowers, who was then sixty-five, and who had a license for single side band radio operation; H.R. and myself, and Connie Jackson, Pete's wife, who was aboard as cook. We made it to Tahiti without anyone jumping ship and without contention or rancor.

The family library may have retained a copy of *A Shoal of Stars*, published by Doubleday in 1967, which gives details of this voyage, in case you want to read more about it. I merely expanded my ship's log to make a book of it.

This adventure was almost totally frivolous, but it was very important to me at the time. For years I tried to figure out why I had insisted on doing it. (Several advisers pointed out that this would be bad for my career, bad for my marriage, a risk to life and limb, and it would set no records, so why was I doing it?) I think I figured out the reason, and it cannot be pictured as noble or possessing any feature that was good for me: I needed to conquer the largest body of water on the planet, and to have my son with me.

I gave some thought, a generation later, to making the same trip with your father, but two things forced a more sensible decision: Your father, by the time he was fifteen, had his own thoughts on what he wanted to do, and they did not include sailing across the Pacific. And second, I would have had considerable opposition to the project from two women — his mother (my daughter) and his grandmother (my wife). I would not have fought them on this. Anyway, I consoled myself with the fact that you can't necessarily go over the same track and recapture the magic.

But what drove this urge to conquer the Pacific? In the summer of 1949, my wife and son and I had a short vacation on Bang's Lake in Illinois. Your grandmother Deirdre was only a few months old and was staying at her grandparents' house in Tampico, Illinois. I had rented a rowboat to which was attached a small outboard motor, a Seagull, with, I believe, a one-and-one-half-horsepower engine. (Do they make anything that weak now?) This boat had no flotation compartments, there were no life jackets aboard. There were oars, which were of course important because of the undependability of the outboard motor.

Bang's Lake is roughly rectangular in shape, stretching from west to east, and fairly shallow for a lake of its size. (I cringe when I think of how safety conscious I have become, along with the times, compared with then. I was twenty-eight and H.R. was four.) I took H.R. with me for the purpose of running to the east end of the lake to see what was over there. Our dock was near the west end. The lake is very shallow, and after we reached about the center of the stretch, the weather thickened, bringing a sudden and stiff east wind, and kicking up a vicious chop. The wind had a long fetch and could make the chop into what seemed like decent surfing waves, and pretty soon I realized that to turn away from the wind and take those waves broadside could swamp the boat. I held it into the wind, but made no headway. Every time I tried to head for shore I ran into the severe risk of broaching or capsizing. I eyed the distance and figured I could make it swimming if I had to, but doubted I could make it carrying a four-year-old. And I had no desire to make it without that four-year-old.

Naturally the engine quit, and I got myself positioned for rowing. The danger mounted as the wind rose, and I got a whiff of panic, which set me toward extravagant promises about the number of candles I would light in appropriate chapels or the way I would restructure my life morally if Providence would see fit to spare me and my innocent son. (Odd thoughts when you consider I am not connected with religious entities that have a lot to do with candles, but fear can push you in strange directions.) After a bit I got the hang of staying into the wind, but off just enough that, staying even with a point on shore, I began to move slowly toward that point, and before we arrived there the wind died down some and I was able to head more directly toward safety. When we docked I was shaking, partly from the cold — we were drenched — and partly from the scare.

I didn't think about it for some years, except that I did know that I had an inordinate fear of rough water. Living only a few blocks from the lake in Chicago, I used to go down to a small beach at night if there were waves, and confront them in the dark. I finally realized I was afraid of being afraid. (President Franklin Roosevelt told the American public once, "The only thing we have to fear is fear itself," and I came to understand what that meant.)

It took a while for me to connect my obsessive desire to navigate my way across the Pacific with a need to overcome this fear — and it would only work if I had my son with me again. There was not much that was rational about this. For one thing, my son, at nineteen, from a marlin-spike seamanship standpoint, was a better sailor than I, and probably looked out for *my* well-being on the voyage; for another, I stacked the cards as much in my favor as I could in planning and executing the trip. I am not suicidal, and consider myself a devout coward when it comes to daring actions. The precautions I took in preventing such annoyances as burning to the water-line, dying of thirst, and sinking to the bottom were impressive. I took along heavy firefighting equipment, extra water in five-gallon jerricans in case the ship's tanks leaked or went bad, inflatable lifeboats and life rafts, and an emergency radio that could deploy a helium-lifted antenna on a long tether and transmit latitude and longitude continuously.

I'm glad I did it. I won't do it again, and I'm not urging you to do it. But if you have a dream of this sort, and can't find noble reasons for insisting on it, don't berate yourself. Sometimes you need to indulge some frivolity, so go ahead.

In doing things for fun it might be wise, however, to exercise some caution in how you treat your frame. I hurt my spine in two places on the Tahiti trip (in the Tuamotu Islands) and had two bouts of corrective surgery, one in late 1965 to remove discs and fuse two vertebrae in the lumbar region and the other in 1968 to relieve what had become chronic pain and the necessity of a neck brace. The surgeons told me then that years later the removal of this bone spur might bring on some traumatic arthritis, and they were right. It started in my seventies and is no worse in my eighties, but it can annoy.

I never cease to feel grateful for what broadcasting did for me. The people I have met and had the privilege of interviewing remain in my memory and surely have given me some perspective on what greatness means. Not everybody I interviewed could be considered great. But the time I spent with Dr. Martin Luther King; presidents Eisenhower, Kennedy, Carter; and heads of state, from Jordan's King Hussein to Spain's Juan Carlos, was important to me.

The year your dad was born I won the only sports trophy I own. I drove in the inaugural race at Ontario, California. We drove Porsche 914-Ss. It was a celebrity pro-am road race and my partner was Mark Donahue. We came in third, beating Paul Newman and Mario Andretti, and the track gave us each a silver bowl inscribed with an account of our accomplishment.

That was the plus side of my motor vehicle year. The downside was that I had a nasty motorcycle accident. I had a BMW that I was bringing back through Cave Creek from a repair shop in Glendale, Arizona. I hit some soft, sandy dirt on a road shoulder. The front wheel dug in and I did an endo that had me cartwheeling through the desert. I suffered a concussion and some cuts and scrapes, and the destruction of the saphenous vein system in my right ankle, plus burns on the leg from tangling with the nubby tire of the rear wheel. I woke up in an ambulance on the way to a hospital. A paramedic was seated beside my stretcher, and I remember saying to him, "I had an accident with my motorcycle." He nodded. I said, "I hope whoever tells my wife lets her know it's not serious." He said, "You've said that several times already." I had taken quite a whack on my helmet, which probably saved my life, and it was a couple of days before I got it all together again mentally. None of my injuries involved broken bones, and I was fully recovered in about six weeks, which is the time it took to get the bike back in shape. While I was in the hospital, members of the *Today* show, of which I was host, sent me a pair of training wheels for my motorcycle.

If I had any advice for you regarding motorcycles it would be to consider that when you are aboard one at high speed, you are the heaviest component of the man-machine complex — and completely exposed; this makes accidents much more damaging to you than if you were in a car.

So now, as your fiftieth birthday approaches, I hope you are satisfied that you are on track, conscious of still being in your prime, and are not in any way depressed about having used up a half century. I also hope you are taking care of your frame and your insides with thoughtful health habits. (Lord, don't you hate a preachy great-grandfather?)

Great-grandfather Norman and
his mother Alma Mae Montee (Nana),
your Great-*great*-grandmother

Sixth Decade:

Fifty to Sixty

What are your feelings about turning fifty? A fiftieth birthday gave me no qualms whatever. I remember that my sixtieth did jar me. There was something about the sixtieth that spelled "old" for me — not the fiftieth and not the seventieth or the eightieth.

In the middle of this decade you have the privilege of reaching middle age. What I call young middle age. I divide middle age into two sections, because in the first decade of this bracket we can go on thinking of ourselves as prime, for the very good reason that we are prime — barring changes and debilities brought on by accident, illness, or neglect of our health, and not counting careers that have required operating physically at the very top edge of muscular strength and precision. ("Prime" for a professional athlete is different from "prime" for a senator.) We should, in the mid-fifties, be able to consider ourselves prime in almost all departments, and superior in matters of judgment, political savvy, business acumen, polished techniques, and accumulated wisdom. And this carries over into prime middle age (starting at sixty-six), where we are more likely to admit not being young anymore.

It has been observed that there are three kinds of aging:

(1) **The chronological,** which is the same for everyone and about which no one can do anything to make it different;

(2) **Wheel of Fortune aging,** which is what fate hands you in the way of genes, conditions, and potential; this is also something you can't take the blame or the credit for; and

(3) **Hands-on aging,** which you can temper and influence — modifying risks, extending and improving, shaping things to your desires (or conversely, hastening decay and dilapidation through abuse and neglect).

If you have inherited congenital

weaknesses of organs or organ systems, or too few telomeres, or propensities for degenerative disorders, then you will need to address these problems, many of which can be dealt with in today's medicine, and by the time you are grown, Xander, there will be much more available in the way of remedy than there has been for my generation. And finally, a healthy lifestyle enhances the probability you'll enjoy a longer life (obvious fact). Not just live longer, but enjoy it. Also, a surefire, guaranteed recipe for living to be a hundred is to eat one cranberry every morning for 36,500 days.

Your world at this stage is bound to have some science and much knowledge that would seem to late-twentieth-century people sheer magic: far more important than the expanding computational ability of machines toward artificial intelligence (this power is doubling roughly every year and by the late twenty-first century will overtake human intellect) will be the coupling of human intelligence — its strengths in pattern recognition, moral concepts, goal and policy constructs — with computers, directing and multiplying the potential, leaving human intelligence, fixed though it is, in charge of machines vastly more intelligent from a rational and computational standpoint. Within your lifetime there may be significant movement toward understanding consciousness.

Nanoengineering will be well under way with many applications in place for medicine. Tiny machines that can repair, manufacture, synthesize, and perform surgical feats will be coming onstage with some rapidity. I think it's possible that both blind and deaf people will, through implants and screen devices worn like glasses, be able to navigate, and read the words of others (through translation of vocal sounds into print); nerve-cell regeneration will be a reality; and paraplegic and quadraplegic victims will no longer be part of the population: their muscles will have been saved from atrophy and restored. Regeneration of brain cells and the ability to arrest and repair chronic brain disorders such as Jakob-Creutzfeldt and Alzheimer's, could either be in place, or showing great promise by the time you are entering middle age.

By the time you are fifty-six, science may be well on the way to synthesizing nutrition from inorganic matter, food that will have the same taste and texture as natural or organic food but not subject to shortage from drought, or distance of transport. All food is made of atoms, and synthetic food, if assembled exactly as biological food, will be indistinguishable.

Human cloning will probably be a reality, after a lot of trial and error and consequent suffering on the part of the flawed creatures put together in various neo-Frankenstein laboratories. It will not have replaced natural reproduction, but seems inevitable in spite of continuing opposition. In the far future it may be a blessing of some sort, but I can't see it now as necessary. (Human cloning is a good example of the grip of the Technological Imperative, which says, "If it can be done it must be done." Why? Do we need a more explosive bomb? Or a human clone? A cure for cancer, yes. An end to birth defects, yes. But, as Wernher von Braun observed, "We need to separate the possible from the permissible.")

By your sixtieth birthday we could hope that some progress will have been made in conflict resolution, because the sophistication of weaponry will certainly continue to increase, outmatching countervailing forces of peacekeeping.

I left the *Today* show in my early fifties, thinking I was leaving television altogether. There were a lot of other things I wanted to do. I started doing them. I wrote two books in that period, which might be in your library (they are now out of print), passed down from your grandmother to your father. I was a visiting fellow at the Center for the Study of Democratic Institutions at Santa Barbara, and your father joined me there once when he was two and staying with us, strolling in a garden on the grounds with the founder, Dr. Robert Hutchins, who had been dean of the Yale Law School when he was twenty-eight and later president of the University of Chicago. The two of them seemed to be in deep philosophic thought.

I sought credentials in two aspects of aging: modest, from an academic standpoint, but they certified the depth of my interest in each field. From Hunter College, with night classes, massive reading lists, and an exam, I got a certificate in social gerontology, and from Mount Sinai School of Medicine, one in geriatric medicine. (I passed an intensive course in geriatric medicine and a board review exam, and it was explained that I could not be board-certified, since I wasn't a physician. The wry humor of this brightens my interest to this day.)

After leaving the regular (and early) routine of hosting *Today*, I had a chance to regroup my faculties and techniques for viewing the world. I got enamored of the wilderness, frequently riding into national parks and forests on horseback. A high point of this activity came when I joined Hubert Yates, who had come out to Arizona with his parents in a covered wagon when he was eight years old, and who was now nearing eighty, to drive a small herd of horses from north of Heber, Arizona, down off the Mogollon Rim, through the Mazatzal Wilderness into Cave Creek. This is a nine-day trip, sleeping on the ground, crossing rivers, and spending many hours in the saddle each day. But I wouldn't trade that trip for added time in an aircraft or on a golf course.

And of course, it's natural to wonder how much wilderness of this sort will still be around when you are the age I was when I enjoyed this long trip — where the scenery was the same as it had been a hundred, a thousand, ten thousand years ago.

Religion in the Post-Postmodern World

I'm predicting the major religions will remain in place, contending with one another on scales and timetables that we never seem able to understand. Historian Will Durant's "indestructible piety of mankind" has served, since long before written history, as a force for good and human advancement, and at the same time has been responsible for unspeakable atrocities and suffering up into present times. Fear of this wildness from fringe elements of religion inspired a bumper sticker of the nineties that read, "Oh God, protect us from people who believe in You." Some cultures have managed to mitigate the evil acts of religious zealots (the best example, I think, is the U.S. Constitution's separation of Church and State), while defending freedom of worship and encouraging religious impulses of compassion and peace.

Theocracies — governments based on religious doctrine — can never be democracies, and at the other end of the spectrum, atheistic governments such as Russian, Chinese, or Albanian communism eventually evolve out of their doctrinaire approach to government to a more humanistic one, or they are eventually overthrown. Theocracy and democracy are mutually exclusive, because such a state is inevitably seized by dictators. Communism destroys hope — and is also inevitably seized by dictators.

I would think that in your second

half century, religion, in the sense of organized, sectarian congregations of worshipers, will still be flourishing, if altered somewhat by broad acceptance of the presence of faiths other than their own. Islam will continue to rise in America, in spite of the unwarranted beating it took after the terrorist attacks of 2001. Mormonism, I would imagine, will have continued in its growth. Christian Protestant sects will have continued to fragment, but demonstrate their durability, not helped by evangelism in the late twentieth century; and Roman Catholicism, in its ancient, glacial flexibility, will probably continue changing at its own pace even into your old age.

I began to think about what all this means when I was young, and my interest in comparative religions and in exploring what my own feelings and beliefs are have tended to grow as the years passed. What attention will you be paying to the subject, if any? I have more to say about this a little later.

The predictions I've made above about this decade of your life may be far afield. But they are what I see at the moment. If they are in any way true, the net result of such change, measuring it against long historic stretches, should see you with a chance for enhanced happiness and security.

Earlier I talked about a possible decline in feelings — esthetic, romantic, enthusiastic — at about this time of life. I learned it need not be permanent, if it happens at all. My overall quality of life was not really diminished, but I experienced a few years of prosaic consciousness where my youth, as I remembered it, had seemed more "poetic." Again, I thought this was the normal course of Nature — a drying up of juices, as one got older.

The first hint of a renewal of a more youthful outlook came when I began to see my marriage in a less pedestrian way. After almost three decades, the years (and Ruth, to a large extent) had helped to shape it as more than satisfactory, but the early change in it involved, first, the inevitable vanishing of novelty. The mystery of a newly loved person melts away as you get to know more and more about that person. If an attraction, imagined to be love, but really only an infatuation, is based solely on this

mystery, it is destined to die — sometimes very early.

If, on the other hand, the compan-
ionship, the affection, the conve-
nience, the mutual respect, the
interdependence, are all high, a marriage can survive the disappearance of
mystery and novelty. But the romance may then be gone.

I don't know how many marriages
manage to rise to a dimension in later
years that puts romance back into the
relationship. But I know some must. I
know one did. I had always appreci-
ated a quality in my wife that it took a
long time to grasp — a depth of character. And I had always been conscious of and grateful for the luck I
had in having someone like that feel
about me as I did about her. As this
characteristic became more evident,

it seemed to provide a new mystery. Where does that dimension come from? Now, again, there were things I did not know or really understand about this person I loved. Pictures of her as a little girl and knowledge that, if we lived long enough, I would see her as an old woman, opened the spectrum of our marriage to expanded volume. Seeing her as a complete human being kindled romantic feelings similar to what I had felt on newly knowing her, but of a wider sort. Added to the initial romantic feelings were impulses of affection very similar to kin concern. This all came back for me simultaneously with a renewed appreciation of the arts, and a realization that my world had drifted for a time into a colorless, practical mode that I might have had to settle for. Whether there is a direct relationship between esthetic sensitivity and a capacity for romantic feelings, I don't know. Maybe it's a coincidence — maybe not. But at present I have no reason to feel I will again lose my connection with this substrate of everything real. As Prince Andrew said: Love.

You may never have to climb out of an arroyo like this, but you should know it can be done.

"Grandee," your grandmother,
on (and at) your father's side

Seventh Decade:

Sixty to Seventy

As I write this part of the letter you are three months old. You smile a lot now and you weigh just over fifteen pounds. And in time you may develop an interest in where you came from. My letter will be a little bit of help. I can't tell you very much beyond five generations back, and neither can anyone else. Some genealogic material may give threads back ten or a dozen generations (such as how you are related to the American frontiersman and Tennessee senator Davy Crockett).

I suppose you will have children, since that seems more likely than not. Your children will probably have children, making you a grandfather, and if at least one of these has a child, you will be a great-grandfather. You might very well get to know that child. Will he or she be able to trace the line back to you, and then to the author of this book, and to your great-*great*-grandmother, living now and privileged to know you? From your great-grandchild to her would be eight generations. If you and your descendants are keen on preserving family lore, and viewing the family tree, it's possible even ten generations could be somewhat known, but beyond that it fades into large numbers and then into the mists of ignorance. And what is ten generations in a line of descent that encompasses at least 7,500 generations back to the beginning of Homo sapiens? Our view of this long path is illuminated by only one spot of light, a spot covering only a handful of generations. This is a tiny window, considering the length of that path.

You will know your mother and father. You will know the generation before them — your grandparents (except for one grandfather, no longer living). You will know all but one of their parents, your great-grandparents. And as we've said, you already know one of your great-great-grandparents and will be told about many of the fifteen others of that generation. You may come to know a little bit about some of the ancestors in the generation before them.

(There were thirty-two of these directly involved in producing you.) So the farther back you go, the more numerous and less known are the forebears. The heritage from any one of them becomes negligible.

Yes, you are related to Davy Crockett. Not descended, but definitely related. Two prongs of research come up with the following line:

Start with you, Alexander William Black. Your father is Cameron Black. His mother is Deirdre Downs, her father is Hugh Downs (me), my father was Milton Downs, his mother was Emma Staub, her mother was Susan Black, her father was James Black, his father was Alexander Black (your name! How about that?), and Alexander married Jane Crockett, whose great-grandfather, Captain Robert Watkins Crockett, had a son John who was the father of Davy Crockett. A bit tenuous, but there really is a connection.

When I was a young boy I was told of the connection and believed it. Then I grew up and didn't believe it. But it was fairly proved to me by a cousin of my father's who did some careful and extensive research into the family background. Crockett was something of a windjammer, and I always felt he threw his life away at the Alamo, but I have had a soft spot in my heart for the old boy since I learned that his quarrel with Andrew Jackson, the one that cost him his Senate seat, was over befriending Native Americans and squatters in western Tennessee; I figured he couldn't be all bad. You can learn more about him in books.

Incidentally, because of the doubling of ancestors every generation, the number of actual people who directly contributed to your genetic makeup back to the time of Davy Crockett's generation is 1,022. These are all ancestors! And they only go back nine generations. Small wonder we can't know a lot about our background beyond a few generations. To go back as far as the beginning of the Christian era, each one of us has far more ancestors than there were people on the earth at that time. Which means you had to have been related to many of these people in more than one way! The human family is really a family.

In this decade you will enter the

prime middle age era. If you experience this transition as I did, you will know (a) that you are noticing some symptoms of being physically older, and (b) it's not bad. All the jokes about aging are based on maladjustment, premature decrepitude, impairment of various kinds, a derisive attitude on the part of the young from ignorance, and deep societal prejudices subscribed to even by the elderly.

In your mid-sixties you will feel inside as you did when you were in your mid-thirties or forties, and will not look a lot different, although you may have gray in your hair and be a little thicker in the middle.

What will your world be like when you run through your sixties? I would suppose that computers (which will probably not be called computers then, but rather something that derives from new physics or nano-technology or robotics — maybe "quants," "nannies," "nano-bots," or some entirely new word) will have become more than mere adjuncts to our intellectual and educational and business functioning. As they have become more and more organic, you and your generation will have become more and more bionic — relying where necessary on remedial joints, artificial lenses, cochlear implants for hearing, kidney aids, circulatory pumps, neural implants for brain and spine, and a whole pharmocopoeia based on chemicals produced in the body rather than from inorganic compounds synthesized in laboratories.

I do not think there will be starships yet. The stars are so far away. But as you grow older, the exploration of our own solar system will have continued by fits and starts, not steadily. Earth problems will retain priority, and scientific research and potential will always be begging for money.

But space is a decent destination, and some progress is inevitable. The sun and its family of planets will continue to be investigated. I should think an expedition to Mars (perhaps more than one) would have taken place by now, after several more unmanned probes. The discovery of earthlike planets in other systems within fifty or so light-years' radius will give us more knowledge about the likelihood of life in other places in the universe. My opinion is that there must be life, however rare, on other worlds. And among places where there is, there must be (even rarer) some equivalent of intellect that may or may not be compatible enough to communicate with us, assuming, with the limiting speed of light, it is close enough to have communication within a meaningful timetable.

I don't even know if you will be interested in stuff like this, but in case you are, you will know my thoughts and feelings on reading this letter, and it will satisfy some of your curiosity about me, if not add to your body of interest. Right now I can't see that your world will have found or communicated with other intelligences. We may quite possibly have established that life exists in other places within the solar system, on one of the moons of one of the giant gas planets, or on Mars — but not intelligence. I would be surprised if we found intelligent life elsewhere in our system. It's hard enough to find it on Earth!

Here is my prediction of two developments in your world in this decade of your sixties: I think quantum computation will by now be established and will open the door to new possibilities for understanding consciousness. Years ago I came to the conclusion that human mental activity is dependent as much on what doesn't happen as what does in the neural circuitry. And quantum computers will deal with the concept of nothing in a way that parallels human thought. (The null factor as a component of consciousness is, to my mind, analogous to the discovery of zero in mathematics. Not much could be done in computation until the zero was added to Arabic numerals. And in the quantum world "nothing" is something. This will show up in quantum computation and add a whole new dimension to investigation.)

The other development is the replacement of the silicon chip with DNA in computers. When the double helix at the core of every living cell is put to work for storage, retrieval, and calculation, it will have moved the element of silicon into retirement and replaced it with carbon. It is not just symbolic that we are carbon-based life. To return to carbon is an act of life, through intellect, and a very significant aspect of evolution. DNA at the core of computers will make the silicon chip look like a stone tablet.

These two things I believe will have forged the character of the middle twenty-first century.

Fortune puts us on a bell curve. At each end of the bell curve is a tiny chance that something might happen. One end is bad news. The other is good news. At one end you might meet with a hideous misfortune like having your whole family wiped out or having your life ended by violence or an act of nature — a random shooting or being hit by lightning. At the other end there is a chance you will win millions of dollars in a lottery, if they still have those things in the second half of your century, and I suppose they will. I am going on the assumption (very strong chance) that your life will be lived in the middle of that bell curve.

And that you will begin to wonder about different things: the size of the universe. What consciousness is. What happens when you die. How much truth there is in certain religious tenets. Why sex begins to slow up a little. Where you left your car keys. Things like that.

There are still other puzzles that you may not ponder (or understand, or be interested in) until you are in your seventies. Remembering my seventies, I struggled with a lot of issues that I thought I had given attention to in earlier years, but realized finally that I had not. In my eighties I began to understand the puzzles — not the solution to the puzzles, but the puzzles themselves. (The view from eighty doesn't always bring instant and complete wisdom. But it gets to be more fun and provides more insight than I had ever thought it could.) Even when you don't have the answer, understanding the question can bring enormous satisfaction. But that's a couple of decades ahead of where you are now.

One of the things I finally did understand was the extent to which mental attitude turns fearsome things into tolerable, and sometimes pleasurable, things.

Alexander, you are descended from a late bloomer. I wish I had learned some tricks earlier than I did (and many people do). How to work. How to take pleasure in organizing such a simple thing as schoolwork. How to remain friendly with people you disagree with. How to give in to someone without losing. How to vent anger without insult. How to derive the ultimate pleasure by sacrificing something for someone else — comfort, money, credit. I did get the hang of all this, sort of, but about a decade later in each case than I should have.

Maybe the most important thing I grabbed out of this decade (sixty to seventy) is what mental attitude can do in the way of mitigating misfortune. The act of putting a good face on something actually has a net effect of making the situation better. So much that is labeled "condition" is really state of mind: Example: When Daniel Boone was an old man, he was interviewed by a reporter who asked him if he had ever been lost in the wilderness. Boone thought a minute and said, "No. I was never lost. Once I was uncertain of my position for four days." Being lost is a state of mind. If you don't think you are lost, you are not lost.

Where are you now, young man, soon to be seventy? What can I tell you now about living that would be of value in your world, so far removed from mine? Only my own feelings and triumphs of the kind that could conceivably be passed on and used by you. Have you by now lost your parents? When your second parent dies you are an orphan, no matter how old you are.

I cannot see you clearly in the misty and diffuse future.

This decade was interesting for me: I became an orphan when I was sixty-one. My father died that year (1982). He was a good man, who solved a lot of mysteries for me. When I was two I remember a black rubber ball he rolled out onto the lawn of a park in Akron, Ohio, where I was born. I would go get it and bring it to him. Maybe he thought I was a dog. But I thought he was a god. Later, as a little boy I thought of him as a king who owned everything, including the moon. Still later he was my protector and a much respected man. When I hit adolescence he was a bit behind the times — didn't wear the right kind of hat; his hat was like a homburg, and the "in" hat was a porkpie — and before I was eighteen he became a complete jerk. A couple of years later he began to recover from this condition and surprised me with some comments that actually made sense. By the time I was in my early twenties he had recovered completely and showed signs of wisdom that I had to admire. Before I was twenty-six he had become again a person worthy of respect, whose opinion was of value to me, and as I look back on him now, he was — not quite a god, but a sort of king, because he had the knack of seeming to believe he owned the world, without any arrogance. He gazed on the human scene with amused detachment, and a kind of wisdom that I still aspire to. I am still indebted to him.

Among the mysteries he explained were two that had really puzzled me. I asked him once what would happen if the immovable object was impinged on by the irresistible force. He disposed of this by pointing out the terms are mutually exclusive: if there exists an immovable object, it by definition precludes the existence of an irresistible force, and vice versa. The other one was the old question, if a tree falls in the forest and there is no one there to hear it, will there be a sound? This too, to him, was simple. He asked me to define "sound." If, he said, sound was merely the expansion and rarefaction of a train of air waves created by the crashing tree, then it didn't matter whether anyone was there to hear it, there would be sound. If, however, sound was the effect of that wave train on an eardrum and the nerves that go into a brain, then if the forest was empty of that eardrum and brain, there would be no sound. He was so wise I used to wonder if he ever puzzled about anything.

The year my father died, 1982, I went to the South Pole. I had wanted to do this for years, and had earlier even involved myself in a syndicated special about Admiral Richard Byrd and his South Pole adventures, but it turned out there was not a sufficient budget to go to Antarctica. We worked around that, focusing on his home in Boston, archive footage, and other biographical material. During the International Geophysical Year (actually parts of 1957 and 1958) it had been determined within about seventy-five yards where the South Pole actually was, and I had seen a photo of a ring of oil drums with the caption that 90 South (the pole) was inside this ring.

But by 1982, with the help of a new polar satellite, scientists were able to determine within twenty *inches* where the earth's axis came out through the ice. That is indeed precision for a globe eight thousand miles in diameter. When I read about this I called John Slaughter, then head of the National Science Foundation, which is in charge of U.S. science in Antarctica, and asked when they were going to move the pole to the corrected position. He said in December. By then I had got the okay from ABC to go, and December is the ideal month, being summer down there. I asked John if he thought I might get to be the one who moved the pole. A week later he called me to tell me the scientists thought it was a good idea.

Dr. Loreen Utz gave me the paperwork showing how they had determined where the pole should really be, and on December 10, at what would be 6:10 p.m. EST, I picked up the South Pole (a fifteen-foot bamboo pole with a tattered green flag on the top) and planted it at the new position, marked by a surveyor's pin. (The Barber Pole, ringed by the flags of the treaty nations, is not really at the Pole but near the Buckminster Fuller geodesic dome, about a quarter mile from where 90 South actually is.) I was able, given the precision of the pole in its new position, and since all meridians converged at the pole, to walk around the pole — around the world — in twenty-four steps, each one in a different time zone.

Grandpa Clyde and Grandma Linda (Granda)
with you and your mom

Eighth Decade:
Seventy to Eighty

You will probably have inherited (or been taught) a work ethic of some sort, but I have a feeling it was different from mine. As I was growing up, it was generally assumed that one should work as an adult at some job or profession until retirement time (age sixty-five), and then, as a reward for your services, you would be turned out to pasture, living on a pension, or Social Security, or the return on investments. This was one of the many assumptions about one's life: I don't remember ever being told by my parents, or anyone else, that I should get a job, or get married, or have children. It just seemed to be something that was in the air; it happened. (And if it didn't happen, it was a circumstance that was considered unfortunate.)

You might, in your eighth decade, find yourself active in a second or third career. You may have decided to plunge into volunteer activities. It is more likely than not that you will have children, and by now, grandchildren.

By the time I was in my seventies, my career in broadcasting had morphed over the years from small-station announcer, to narrator and newscaster, to game show host, to broadcast commentator, and to anchor of a TV multisubject hour. After leaving all that in a stab at retirement, I turned to occasional irregular broadcast projects, appeared as a guest on talk shows, or substituted for network anchors, embarked on academic lecturing, and did commentaries on the Internet. But nothing that I could call another career.

I have made an effort to carve out some real leisure time, but this was slow in coming. I was close to eighty when the house we built in Paradise Valley, Arizona, was completed and I carried my bride of fifty-five years across the threshold, and expected the leisure to begin in earnest.

And then a full year went by before I got on a horse or got out to the glider port to fly my glider. What was wrong with this picture? Probably nothing — only that I complained about it. There being no slavery or indentured servitude in our country, I had no one to blame but myself for this situation. I love writing, and speaking, and reading, and participating in intellectual discussions (in the hope, I suppose, that intelligence is contagious). I was constantly on the go, unable to relax. We did squeeze in movies and we dined out with friends, and we traveled some, but we were not like other people we knew who were retired. People to whom golf is a religion play golf when they retire. The truly peripatetic spend most of their time on cruise ships. Some others entertain all the time, or frequent arenas and ball fields covering spectator sports.

Your great-grandmother and I do some of this, but a lot of our enjoyment consists of activities that I regarded when I was young as somewhat dull: reading in silence, or to each other, listening to recorded music, sometimes watching TV or rented movies — on occasion just experiencing the transition from sunset to night.

At age seventy-three, I started rereading the Great Books of the Western World and should finish them after ten years. This, at a speed of fifteen pages a day, leaving plenty of opportunity to read other things. I started on December 10, 1994, fifty years to the day from when I embarked on the original list.

However, the appeal of these activities has not dulled our zest for adventure: exploring tributaries of the Amazon, snowmobiling in the White Mountains, visiting field sites for UNICEF in Kenya, Egypt, China, and Nicaragua, going to the North Pole on a Russian icebreaker, are things we do or have done together. We finally did a joint lecture for Arizona State University on the subject of marital longevity. I think they thought we were some sort of experts, being married at that time fifty-eight years. Our newest adventure has been taking care of you, an activity of great pleasure, which evokes memories of when your father was an infant, and farther back to when his mother was. When you were a few weeks old, we were reflecting on the technological changes since your mother was a baby. Disposable diapers, requiring no safety pins, virtually no diaper services anymore, portable intercoms between the baby's room and its parents', the range of strollers and cribs and chairs and toys — people born today find themselves in a much more varied and colorful world.

I feel certain that however different your world will be when you are this age (over seventy), people will still feel intense pleasure in watching the majestic diurnal wheeling of the planet — producing twilight from sunset, and night from twilight. Sometimes I say to myself, "At this time of day, at this time of the year, at this time of life, perfection is very close." It helps, I'm sure, if you are in harmony with yourself.

If you develop health problems, I would imagine a lot more of them will be solvable in your lifetime than were in mine — although I consider myself lucky in having encountered, so far, only things that are correctible. I have been somewhat ashamed that I don't have a Heisman Trophy to show for ruined knees, but over the years, through a series of accidents, I did manage to ruin them. I was in an auto accident in 1948, hit by a retired police captain (not in a police car), which sprung the passenger door open and threw my pregnant wife out onto the pavement. This alarming collision (which could have resulted in your never having been born) turned out not to be harmful to your great-grandmother or your yet unborn grandmother. My left knee was injured, but it was minor and I felt I recovered from it completely. I had always had the idea that injuries of any kind may do damage, but that they would leave no residual deterioration. You got injured, you got well. It was that simple.

It isn't that simple. And after coming off a horse on an off-trail ride and landing on my knee on a stump, getting whacked on the kneecap by a golf ball right off the head of a driver, running down thirty-four flights of stairs in a New York apartment building in a race with your father, who was about ten at the time, and a few other indiscretions and follies, I began to see that knee injuries don't just get well on their own.

I tend to be a denyer. This is not all bad. I tried to avoid the word "painful." I said my knee condition was "annoying." I did not want to believe the condition was (a) irreversible, (b) painful, (c) something that could diminish the quality of my life. The result was that, toward the last, if I walked six blocks in Manhattan, I found it "annoying" enough that I was ready to sit on the curb and wait for a cab.

The combination of cartilage erosion and traumatic arthritis finally forced me to the conclusion that my knees were shot, and I'd better do something about it. In 1993 I had an arthroscopic procedure on the worst one (my right), and it bought me some time. It cleaned out debris and eased some of the discomfort, but the surgeon told me at the time that eventually I would need total joint replacement — most likely on both knees. He was right.

Not wanting to go through two recovery periods, I elected to have both knees replaced at the same time. I knew I needed to do this, and asked to have my absence from *20/20*, the TV show I was hosting, explained by their simply saying I was away. But the executive producer, Victor Neufeld, said, "Why don't you go public with this? You might do some good." I went along with his suggestion and have been glad I did. The operation and a lot of the recovery were covered by the program, certainly the most personal project I ever aired on national TV. Many people who needed new knees have contacted me to tell me they are glad they went ahead with replacement. The people who have been dissatisfied with the results are mostly a handful who, when asked if they followed the exercise regimen after surgery, said, "Well, I know I was supposed to, but it was too painful (or inconvenient)." It is very important to do the exercises afterward. Atrophied quadriceps muscles come back amazingly, and if you don't do the exercises you will be left with legs you can't get fully straight, and can't bend very far.

I went back on the air thirteen days after surgery. I was back in the field in four months and in ten months I could run upstairs — something I hadn't done for twelve years before the surgery, the deterioration was so bad. I am fond of saying, "These are the good old days of medicine."

I burden you with this tale because, although my contribution to your makeup is small (one-eighth), great-grandchildren do inherit some physical characteristics, and should you do damage to your knee joints, medical science will surely by then have developed some noninvasive method of growing your own new cartilage right in the joint.

Will what we think of as progress in my generation continue to accelerate in yours, as it has during my lifetime? The first powered flight was in 1903 and by 1969 we had put men on the moon. The acceleration was breathtaking. Can you progress at this rate through the twenty-first century, and if you do, what will it bring? I can guess, but it may make you smile.

I think your generation will have wrestled the problem of overpopulation to the ground, and will have established an economy based on service rather than growth. Growth, in terms of more people, more resources taken from the earth's crust, more manipulation of material, is doomed. It's still possible to grow, in knowledge, in life enhancement, in the expansion of space frontiers (space offers extensive reprieve from the limits to growth), and in the next steps in scientific methodology. If your cohorts and colleagues have not moved in this direction, there is a very good chance you will not have a quality life.

But again, I go on the assumption that humanity tends to do that which ensures its continuance, and so I try to see you as a comfortable, successful, happy individual in a world more glorious than I can envision. Your seventies should be even better than mine were.

In my eighth decade (seventy to eighty) I had some gratifying experiences, again opened to me because of broadcasting. I dove on an eleven-hundred-year-old wreck off the Turkish coast in 1992. A marine archaeology team had discovered it in 1990 and had carefully staked out the ruins of a merchant ship carrying amphorae — probably of wine. It had gone down in about 125 feet of water quite close to shore, which was a cliff. This was in the Mediterranean, not the Black Sea side of Turkey. What made it special for me was that I was permitted to bring up some of the amphorae. These and other, heavier pieces of the cargo were attached to inflated bags, which offset their weight and made it easier to get them to the surface. The romantic notion that these held wine that would be beautifully preserved and aged, and of exquisite taste, is, I'm afraid, fanciful. They contained sludge, long since gone from sour to vinegar, and then to a compound comprising the clay of the inside of the vessel and seawater, along with whatever fermented grape juice had been there at the beginning. (The year 891 was not necessarily a great year.)

The dive had a feature I had never seen before: In order to allow a little extra bottom time without a diver having to go into decompression, the line up to the surface, at about eighteen-feet depth, had a station to which were tied air tanks with regulators and books — actual paperback books — so that you could switch to a different tank and save your personal air, and while letting whatever nitrogen you had dissolved in your bloodstream gradually dissipate, keeping you from getting the bends, you could read. Some of the books were beginning to disintegrate. Seawater is not friendly to pulp paper. But some of them remained readable. It was restful to hang there in an underwater library, relaxing and enjoying the warmer water (at about ninety feet down there was a thermocline below which the water was icy). We would avoid the bends and enrich our literary lives at the same time, floating at the eighteen-feet level. Luckily, most of the books were in English.

I also did a lot of soaring in this decade. I love taking people up who have never been in any aircraft before and letting them experience the thrill of flying without an engine, and (if they are willing) taking the controls and tumbling through the sky. The glider I have is a Grob Acro, and it is so stable — it just wants to fly — that there is no attitude a passenger could put it into that I could not recover from. Upside down, on its side, half a loop — whatever. I've talked to commercial airline pilots who glide as a hobby, and they agree it is much more fun than powered flight. Certainly more fun than presiding over a battery of computers in a commercial airliner.

In the summer of 1998, Ruth and I had an opportunity to go to the North Pole on a Russian icebreaker. The Explorers Club, of which I've been a member for a quarter century, mounted this expedition and it became a broadcast project, with finished footage I aired on *20/20*.

I believe that since tourism there started just before you were born, by the time you are in your twenties, a steady stream of tourists will be visiting both poles and ocean depths like where the *Titanic* sank, and I'm pretty sure there will have been tourists visiting a space station when you were still a young man. If you chose to become an astronaut, you might have already become an early visitor to Mars.

When I was seventy-two the great

cellist Yo-Yo Ma said to me during an interview on the PBS program *Live From Lincoln Center*, "I hear you are a composer. If you write something for cello, I'll play it." This made my hair stand on end. I don't know where he had heard I was a composer, and the last time I had written for a large orchestra was when I was twenty-seven. This was a prelude in the nature of an elegy, which was published and is still occasionally performed, bringing me royalty checks every year ranging from $14 to $40-some! (I'd hate to have to live on what I make from writing orchestral music.) But I started on the cello piece. I did not get this finished till I was eighty, but he liked it and premiered it with the St. Louis Symphony that May. Your great-grandmother Ruth and I went to St. Louis and attended the concert, and were gratified that the audience seemed to like it and that a critic with a reputation of being harsh spoke well of it in the newspaper.

Probably the most fun I've had broadcasting was covering John Glenn's return to space when he was seventy-seven. John Glenn was the first American to orbit the earth, solo in a Mercury capsule, in 1960. Glenn promised me that *20/20* could be the magazine to do the story of his return to space as a mission specialist on the shuttle STS 75. I first contacted him while he was still a senator and it had not yet been decided whether he would go. NASA said we could not take cameras in and videotape or film Glenn's training. This was a blow, but I had to agree with NASA that to let us in would necessitate letting the press in generally, and that would be damaging to his training.

My producer, Rob Wallace, went to NASA and said, "Downs is the same age as Glenn. Could we tape *him* doing the training?" They said yes, if I qualified physically. When I qualified we started, and while I did none of this at the same time Glenn was doing it, I went through hypoxia and explosive decompression maneuvers, and spent time in the gutted 707 they use for weightless practice (nicknamed the "Vomit Comet" since some people get very ill in weightlessness).

I had done this years before at Wright-Patterson Air Force Base in Dayton, and all told had forty-eight

minutes (in thirty-second increments) in weightlessness. Having
practically qualified, I had a whiff of
disappointment at not being able to
go, or at least be a backup for Glenn.
But I was not an astronaut.

When the mission was over and he
had landed at the Cape, I said to
Glenn, "If, ten years from now,
NASA wants to see how eighty-
seven-year-olds do in space, let's
both go." He said, "You're on." It is
of course more than likely that both
his wife and mine would show some
resistance to this. His family was
against his going that time. But on
that mission Glenn did a lot for the
United States space program, for a
better understanding of aging, and
for geriatric medicine itself.

Your ninth decade will be launched

in the year 2082. You will have helped your grandchildren grow up and should make ready for great-grandchildren. I can tell you that this is an extremely gratifying stage of life.

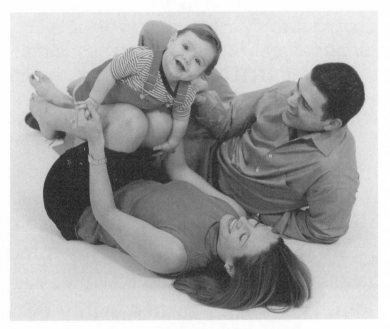

Your parents Nikki and Cameron
(really Mommy and Daddy)

Ninth Decade:

Eighty to Ninety

So now you have the view from eighty. Somehow, eighty in my mind has always stood for a crowning wisdom, and when I turned eighty I expected to wake up that day vastly wiser than I had ever been. (Maybe I didn't really expect it. But I sort of hoped for it.) The truth is, unless you're a complete dunderhead, some wisdom will come out of the accumulated experiences and observations you've had during the years. And it doesn't hurt that some people will tend to regard you as wise, simply because of your age. This is a terrible mistake on their part, because a human can become simply old without really maturing. Sometimes a young jerk will grow up to be an old jerk. It requires some discrimination on the part of younger people to make the distinction. The brighter ones do. But the idea that age automatically breeds wisdom is refreshing in that it represents a sort of reverse ageism. This doesn't completely offset the prejudices we still retain in our society.

In the middle of your ninth decade you joined the young old (the fifteenth of my seventeen stages of life). You will probably still see yourself as middle-aged. When you are eighty-nine you will join the old old. Maybe then the man looking back at you from the mirror will definitely look as though he's been around for a lot of years.

Your world, I trust, will still be intact, and will be a place for you to enjoy life, even if you worry about your descendants. People always do. I hope you have not become a sour person who is convinced oncoming generations are going to hell — dismantling civilization because of their music or mores or the length of their hair or their fashions or their increasing nudity, or, in a reverse swing of the pendulum, their reactions to all of the above. Humanity does these things. The only thing that really counts is: Are you, personally, fair, compassionate, true to yourself? You will have earned peace and satisfaction. Someone said, "We bargain for happiness and settle for peace." I don't feel that way. If you are blessed with that modicum of luck, and have worked at fashioning yourself into a person of integrity, you can have happiness along with peace even if the world is not peaceful — and it probably won't be.

The ultimate heroism, a philosopher said, "is to know the world as it is, and love it." I suppose this is, at root, a religious idea. You can love the world in innocence, blind to how awful a lot of it is; or you can have a tight grip on reality, and find yourself turning bitter and despairing. How can you have it both ways? It takes a deep spring of almost mystical vitality to face the way things are and still be free of hatred and fear — to care about this place and all life in it.

So now I'm old enough as I write this to risk talking about religion, because you are old enough when you read it to understand what I'm saying. You may not be in agreement with all of it, but your own ideas, whatever they are, while certainly individual, might roughly parallel mine. (This is my application of the "great minds run in the same channel" theory.)

I have said that I believe, like Thomas Carlyle, that "There is one True Church, of which at present I am the only member." I have had trouble all my life with religious dogma. Dogma, I admit, have seemed to serve as a kind of mortar that makes religious sects self-coherent. So maybe they have a role.

Will Durant wrote that the tragedy of religion is that if unorganized it languishes, and if organized, it suffers corruption. Most details of most religions I find too dogmatic to be acceptable. However, when looked upon as allegorical, a lot of various scriptural stories and parables are meaningful and beautiful.

I am not an atheist. To me, atheism is a dogmatic religion. A dedicated atheist has a firm belief, to which he clings as tenaciously as a fundamentalist clings to his belief in fundamentalism. And atheism's major flaw is that it tries to prove a negative. Thus it does violence to logic. Science will never prove that there is a God. Nor that there isn't.

I find — maybe it has to do with how I was brought up — that there are elements of the Christian religion (not as applied or organized through the ages but as it has survived in its essence) that contain deep truths. The survival of this essence is a tribute to a thread that has run through good times and bad.

Through the Dark Ages it was the monasteries that preserved classical antiquity for us, and kept alive, almost in secret, the basic teaching of the founder, which put less emphasis on faith than on charity — a significant aspect of the religion, in my mind.

The only strong feelings I have that might be linked to a religious outlook are of overwhelming gratitude at being favored with such a good life. If people who have been dealt a bad hand — people who suffer, physically or mentally, or are the victims of great tragedy — can manifest real faith, it would be pathetic if I couldn't feel something along that line, considering my fortunate circumstances.

You may have achieved a solid sense of security without any formally religious faith. Or you might have a formal faith that is unshakable, and invulnerable to the arguments of others. In our country the separation of Church and State is the greatest friend organized religion has. It protects people's right to worship or not as they choose, and it protects worshipers from state interference with their practice.

At this time of your life, I should imagine that a great deal of human thinking will be enhanced and amplified by machine intelligence. Many years ago Norbert Wiener, who coined the word "cybernetic" from a Greek word meaning "steersman," cautioned that if we humans abdicate our responsibility, we will wind up working for the machines. His warning presupposes that we and the machines will remain entirely separate, and in adversarial positions. I don't think this is how the scenario will play out.

Many science fiction writers have written stories about "cyborgs" — cybernetic organisms, part protoplasm and part cybernetic machines (i.e., part human and part computer). In your old age you may see cyborgs. You will most likely be partially bionic, and be on the way to becoming a cybernetic organism yourself. If you have, as I have, metallic joint replacement, artificial lenses implanted in your eyes, or any prosthetic devices or organ-assist mechanisms, you are already partially bionic. Neural implants to enhance brain function may be available in your seventies or eighties. I can't see anything sinister in this. It will probably just be part of evolution.

The only thing that counts is, will full-blown cybernetic organisms be capable of love and enjoyment? Do they have a reasonable chance of coping with accident and suffering? Can they help one another? Will they retain the kind of consciousness that can worship and feel thanks for the majestic unfolding of this universe, which in its immensity makes us feel, as Sir Arthur Eddington said, we are "citizens of no mean city"? Will there be enough retention of their humanity to prevent their merely extinguishing the human race? (My hope that the answer to this is yes merely shows my own chauvinism — my desire that human life continue as human.)

You and your dad in very high humidity!

Tenth Decade:

Ninety to One Hundred

At this point I have no personal history to give you, or advice based on experience, since I have not lived this decade. However, I have some thoughts about what it might be like — both for you and me, if we make it, and for the planet — based mostly on extrapolating trends. We have to acknowledge that the personal journey ahead will involve fighting a rearguard action — knowing that physical changes are now pretty much a one-way street. This would be sad and depressing if that were all there was to life.

If you have been fortunate enough to avoid certain kinds of mental shipwreck, there are some interesting qualities of mind that can, I believe, make these years satisfying and more than pleasant. Tall order?

The mind, in addition to providing you with consciousness and volition, divides itself into two parts: the cognitive — that part that does all your figuring out, your logical calculations — and another part that is a home for your emotional-intuitive life. This part has a spiritual root, and I suspect has the capacity to allow you peace and joy, not only in the face of inevitable physical decay, but as a scaffolding for support of your self, *even if you are overtaken by mental shipwreck.*

I'll get to that deep thought in a moment, but first I want to comment on the meaning of the word intellectual. This is a noun applied to people who enjoy exercising their cognitive machinery. Your grandmother (my daughter) accuses me of being an intellectual. And she has said she means by that — by the term "intellectual" — one who gets his grip on reality through the rational portion of his mind, as opposed to someone who grasps reality through the emotional-intuitive portion. If this is the case, I plead guilty to being an intellectual. An intellectual is not necessarily intelligent. It's just that his connection with the world is maintained by his thinking processes. This has inclined me to the materialist-reductionist approach to scientific (and some other) truths. But it has not closed all other avenues of thought, or left me blind to some spiritual truths. In my eighties I learned that it is possible to have a sense of spiritual truth while being agnostic.

Peace and joy do not automatically come to (or stay with) everyone who accumulates years. But there are instances — some of them, strangely, under conditions of mental impairment. Garson Kanin wrote a beautiful book called *A Thousand Summers* in which a man, suffering dementia, relived a summer affair, an idyllic episode when he was young. He relived this not once, but over and over. He was deliriously happy for years. This kind of mental disorder, which ushers a person into a world of his own making, where he can be anyone he wants to be — Napoleon, Elvis, whatever — may mark the end of an effective life, but it appears to be free of suffering. Other disorders of the mind can be cruel. But underneath it all is the reality of personhood, and Nature may prove kind enough to provide some liberation from the anguish of initial disintegration. (And maybe I'd have to experience it to know whether I am right or wrong about this.)

But if you have to lose your mind, hope for the fork in the road that takes you to dementia praecox, and try to avoid paranoid schizophrenia. The one is a kind of paradise, the other real hell. I suspect there will be methods and chemicals for dealing with these conditions in marvelous ways when you are in your nineties, ways that reduce suffering. And of course, it is not inevitable that you will go dotty just because you are old. There are many very old people who have not had strokes or Alzheimer's, and if the brain remains undamaged by injury or disease, it does its job with almost the efficiency it had when it was younger.

I have come to believe that when it becomes too troublesome or difficult to get on a horse, or don scuba gear or hike a mountain trail, or when through loss of muscle mass or arthritis mobility is curtailed, there is still a lot of music to listen to, a lot of books to read, and contemplative activities that can go a long way to make up for loss of physical vigor. Only chronic intractable pain or sudden and complete loss of independence (having to ground oneself from driving, or worse, loss of ability to see or walk unaided) could cut into happiness. Even then, we can hope that techniques for accommodation and adjustment might allow us to face shrinking horizons without fear. There's some valiance in fighting rearguard actions. Since my conviction that this hope is reasonable does not come out of personal experience, it is less impressive, but it is no less firm.

Technology in your tenth decade will have produced marvels that would probably boggle the mind of anyone from my generation. Fossil fuels will surely be virtually exhausted by now. Certainly they will have become so expensive that alternative energy sources will have over-taken them: wind and tide, extensive gathering fields for solar energy, hell-power (the tapping of magma that makes volcanoes) — all will have been developed and deployed. With these and some other energy sources that are renewable, it will have become possible to separate the hydrogen from the oxygen in water and convert to a hydrogen economy, as it was called in the late twentieth century, at which time it was understood that the energy necessary to produce hydrogen in quantity would be more than the energy you'd get back out by burning it. Burning it, of course, produces water. When you burn something you combine it with oxygen, and hydrogen combined with oxygen is: water! A very clean ash. But the hydrogen will have to be procured through abundant nonpolluting sources of energy before we can speak of a hydrogen economy.

Much more crucial to the world's economy than oil will be water. And with enough nonpolluting energy, usable water will again become available at reasonable cost. Desalinization, costly and energy-intensive at first, should by now have become a practical technology.

If you reach this decade you will see (maybe participate in) debates about the extent to which computers are correct in their claim of being conscious. Genetic engineering will have modified life to a great extent. Nutrition will have been synthesized from inorganic matter, and the killing of animals for food will be a thing of the past. (Leonardo da Vinci once said that he believed the time would come when humans would find it morally wrong to kill other animals to eat them.)

- Life expectancy and life span will both have gone up: better medical knowledge and health habits will have brought expectancy up over a hundred, and human life span may have been altered through methods of slowing cell metabolism, reducing oxidation, transmitting information from the nucleus of one cell to the daughter cell with greater accuracy, cutting down on the noise-to-information ratio, enhancing cellular repair mechanisms, and lightening the load of organ systems with implanted computers and nanopumps. Life span could be raised by several decades, and that would mean some people could live to be 160 to 180, and ninety-year-olds would be like twentieth-century sixty-year-olds.

• Of course in the end, entropy will defeat any living being, and physical immortality will not be achieved. The Second Law of Thermodynamics, which inexorably moves systems from order to chaos, cannot be disobeyed. And longer life span will bring great challenges to humanity. I think it will be the cause of severe social disruption.

What kind of music might you be listening to in your nineties? There are bound to be some changes. Probably the better folk music will survive into these years, and if Harold Schonberg, onetime music critic of *The New York Times* was right, four hundred years from now, Bach, Brahms, Handel, Beethoven, and a few others will still be in the classical repertoire, and much of the modern and postmodern music will have been consigned to the dustbin.

Will the gap in taste from one generation to the next persist in popular music? I think it is very likely. My brother Wallace (your great-great-uncle) had a discussion at the dinner table one time with his thirteen-year-old daughter, who asked him, "Daddy, what kind of music did they listen to when you were alive?" He said it dampened his whole day.

Will the diatonic scales we use now be divided further into quarter tones? If the brain (maybe by now a computer-assisted brain) could sort that out, and not simply dismiss those tiny pitch differences as "out of tune," some extremely complicated music could result, and something akin to the symphony could be brought back in glory. This would be a bigger breakthrough than Bach's tempering the scale.

Will you make it to one hundred? (Have you already made it to one hundred, and are reading this right now and smiling?)

In my lifetime, you had a fifty-fifty chance of living to age seventy-four (if male, seventy-nine if female).

Actually, a special panel of the Social Security Advisory Board determined in 2003 that we have underestimated life expectancy, and that by the time you are twenty-seven (in 2029) life expectancy for men will be seventy-seven. On reaching seventy you have an even chance of making it to about eighty-six. So your life expectancy will always be up ahead of your age, but in shrinking increments. It has been observed that everyone dies short of his life expectancy. There's always a chance you'll have some added time.

There are more than sixty thousand centenarians in our country as I write this. About one in four thousand people reaches the age of a hundred. If you want to bet on reaching 110, you will do much better at the average slot machine. And your chances of winning a national lottery jackpot of $60,000,000 are vastly greater than living to the full span of 122 — I base this number on the only life documented to have gone that long — or possibly 125, if the claim of Habib Miyan of Jaipur, India, is valid. He did retire in 1938, and his pension card shows he collected every year since then. He apparently was born in 1878. He is a Muslim and wants to make a hajj to Mecca. His age, as you read this, will either have been authenticated or disproved.

Okay, you made it to one hundred. As long as we're fantasizing, let's look at the next decade.

Hang in there, Xander!

Eleventh Decade:

100 to 110

In this decade you are, of course, firmly in the seventeenth stage of life. You qualify as an ancient.

About ten years before you were born I interviewed a number of centenarians who participated in a University of Georgia study. They were the cream of the crop, because the study was not about disease and impairment so much as trying to find out what changes there were in healthy people that old. These people, men and women, ranged in age from 102 to 106, and like any other age group, varied widely among themselves. But they had a couple of things in common: not one of them was bitter, or hate-filled, or complaining. I wondered if that had something to do with their longevity. And while they were mentally agile, and in some cases quite sharp, none of them was physically robust. You do not reach one hundred (or for that matter, eighty) and embark on a career as a star athlete.

One member of this group was a woman named Mary Elliott, who, the morning that I was to interview her, lost her daughter, who was almost eighty. When we found this out from her son-in-law we immediately backed off and said we did not want to burden her with an interview at a time like this. She, however, insisted that we go ahead with the interview, saying that if she canceled it, it would be dishonoring her daughter's memory. So we went ahead and set up the interview.

She spoke movingly of her child, saying that she had been asked to give back to God the marvelous gift he had given her all those years before. I found her a remarkable woman for many reasons, and corresponded with her for four years. Her memory was excellent and she could articulate facts and ideas and philosophies with as much skill as much younger people.

The university frequently sent doctors to examine the participants in the study, and Mary told me that one time, when the medical team came to her house, she wanted to give them refreshments. She said it surprised her when one of them would say he couldn't have anything with milk in it because of lactose intolerance, and another couldn't eat the deviled eggs because of cholesterol. She said to me, "I eat anything I want."

We wrote to each other about every other month. She had views on world affairs, music, humor, and aspects of the university's study of people her age. I learned from this that while frailty is inescapable in advanced age, mental deterioration is not. Brain tissue, along with muscle tissue, shrinks. We lose some as time goes by. You will have lost upward of 20 percent by the time you're ninety-five. But since we only use about 20 percent of the brain to begin with, and since memory and a lot of brain activity is holistic — that is, it takes place in more than one part of the brain — and since the slowing of both neuron firing and the neurotransmitter activity responsible for recall and connecting symbols generally can be offset by acquired techniques of thinking and accumulated wisdom — you have something that for a long time can act as a countervailing force to mental deterioration — this can result in the same mental sharpness a person has at a much younger age.

Since the appearance of human intelligence a few dozen millennia ago, and of technology a few hundred years ago, the rate of technical advancement, and the ability of our form of life to alter the environment — for good or ill — have been accelerating in a way that makes it impossible even to imagine what changes will occur in the next few millennia.

There is an exquisite razor's edge, though, which seems to balance, delicately, on whether we will save ourselves by colonizing space and moving out to the stars, or screw up completely and ruin this fragile planet, which is right now the only place we have to live. If the latter scenario is the future, there is no future — for humanity. And we will then have joined countless other species that marched into extinction as cosmic time plods on.

Is this of any moment to you and me, Xander? Only if you have inherited the same weird temperament that finds pleasure in thinking about such things.

Evolution may have been a blind-chance force up to the time it produced us, but we humans have seized the reins of evolution and it is a different ball game now. The fact that we were given this intelligence has a theistic flavor to it.

A great part of my theology, such as it is, has to do with the way in which we were given control of, and responsibility for, the future of life. This is an awful charge. But that is the challenge of being human. Again I am grateful even for that challenge.

I stated earlier that while my beliefs are fairly fluid, my faith is solid. There is a difference between faith and belief. If you believe something that others can prove wrong, your belief is not something you can trust. For example, if you deeply believe the earth is flat (and there are people who want to believe this), you will come to grief or lose your mind when confronted with the many mutually reinforcing proofs that the world is spherical. My faith in God is not dependent on anything science or logic points to.

And logic, by its own rules, is not airtight. Basic flaws appear when logic applies some of its own rules. One famous example is the statement by a Chinese that "All Chinese are liars" (with the implication that anything he says, since he is Chinese, is a lie), produces a paradox. If his statement is true then he has just lied. Therefore the statement is false, but if it is false, then he has not lied and the statement is true, and we are plunged into infinite regression.

Subjective truths escape the errors of logic and the limitations of science. Faith is of the fabric of subjective truth.

Let me give an example of subjective truth: if you and I are in an argument about whether infant mortality is higher in Mississippi than in Massachusetts, one of us is right and the other is wrong. Research can find out which one of us is right. But now imagine an argument about whether I prefer horseback riding to scuba diving, or the other way around. I know which I prefer, and no amount of argument, no amount of library or field research, can have any connection with a truth that I *know*. Religious faith has its roots in this realm.

Religious *beliefs,* however, are vulnerable.

Years ago I saw a cartoon in *The New Yorker* magazine where two young women in a coffee shop were discussing a third. One of them was saying, "Well, Joan is not really happy. She just *thinks* she is." Happiness is self-defining. If you think you are happy, you are happy. Real religious faith is like that.

I wish you a good life, however long it is. I wish your descendants contentment, and I hope that you will know them for a few generations. There is great happiness in that, I can testify.

If you are reading this as an old man, I feel privileged to have talked to you across a gulf of time. If you wish that you could talk to me across the same gulf, don't fret about it.

Talk to your descendants. Time only goes in one direction. They will appreciate your taking the time to send some words to them.

I have certainly enjoyed getting these words to you.

I have enjoyed getting to know you, and hope I can watch you grow up.

I have enjoyed everything.

Be well.

Hugh Downs
(your great-grandfather
on your father's mother's
side — Poppy)
Arizona, midyear 2003

Your parents and your great-grandparents
(Gammy and Poppy) very soon
after you arrived

About the Author

Hugh Downs is one of the most recognized figures in American television. He coanchored ABC's *20/20*, hosted NBC's *Today* show for nine years, and was Jack Paar's sidekick for five years on NBC's *Tonight Show*. He received multiple Emmy Awards throughout his career and is the author of nine books.